THE
LOYALTY
FACTOR

BUILDING TRUST
IN TODAY'S
WORKPLACE

THE
LOYALTY FACTOR

BUILDING TRUST IN TODAY'S WORKPLACE

Carol Kinsey Goman, Ph.D.

MasterMedia Limited
New York

Library of Congress Cataloging-in-Publication Data

Goman, Carol Kinsey.
  The loyalty factor: building trust in today's workplace/Carol Kinsey Goman.
    p.   cm.
  Includes bibliographical references.
  ISBN 0-942361-29-6 (pbk.)
  1. Trust (Psychology).   2. Confidence.   3. Loyalty.   4. Management.
  I. Title.
  HD38.G6285   1991
  658'.001'9—dc20   90-63423
                                                               CIP

Designed by Stanley S. Drate/Folio Graphics Co. Inc.

Manufactured in the United States of America

10   9   8   7   6   5   4   3   2   1

*To Skip,
my husband and best friend,
who makes loyalty easy.*

CONTENTS

1 | AN OVERVIEW

2 | THE EMPLOYEES' AGENDA

3 | MANAGING FOR LOYALTY

4 | A CULTURE FOR LOYALTY

5 | THE NEW LOYALTY

ACKNOWLEDGMENTS

Many people have contributed to the creation of this book. First of all, I want to thank everyone who allowed me to query them through questionnaires and personal interviews. In addition, I want to express my special gratitude to Signe Wilkinson, whose cartoons have enhanced so many of my efforts, and Susan Stautberg, whose vision brought it all together.

INTRODUCTION

This book is designed for managers who want to influence their people in ways that develop a stronger sense of unity and purpose.

Modern life in all its complexity creates a feeling of isolation. Meaningful involvement in our work and working relationships can provide the rewarding sense of belonging. Most of us learned about group participation and commitment in our early homelife and school activities. The importance of belonging, contributing, and being loyal is easily recognized. In this book I will introduce ways that management can utilize an increased understanding of loyalty in the workplace to gain the trust of employees, and to bond them to a common goal.

This book is about adjusting to change.

The relationship between employees and management is changing from one based on a long-term agreement to one which addresses the temporary nature of most business liaisons. Loyalty has not necessarily disappeared from the business relationship, but it is manifesting differently under the new paradigm. Those managers who understand the changing dynamics of organizational loyalty, and learn how to apply those understandings, are developing a key management skill.

This book will expose you to a cutting-edge national issue which hasn't yet appeared on the national agenda.

My national research shows uniform concern and deep interest from both employees and management struggling with the implications of the changes in organizational loyalty. Some corporations and managers have well-developed strategies for building loyalty. But most upper and middle managers have never taken the time to adequately examine the issue of loyalty and the ways in which employee commitment is affected by management policies and new marketplace realities.

This book will help you place organizational loyalty in a context congruent with your employees' other loyalties.

Loyalty to an organization does not have to mean disloyalty to other important parts of life. A new definition of loyalty allows for balance among multiple loyalties, including family, personal ethics, and overall career goals. Properly positioned so that all loyalties enhance one another, organizational loyalty profits the individual as well as the company.

THE
LOYALTY
FACTOR

BUILDING TRUST IN TODAY'S WORKPLACE

1 | AN OVERVIEW

EXAMINING ASSUMPTIONS

One night at sea, the ship's captain saw what looked like the lights of another ship heading toward him. He had his signalman blink to the other ship: "Change your course ten degrees south." The reply came back: "Change your course ten degrees north." The ship's captain answered: "I am a captain. Change your course south." To which the reply was: "Well, I am a seaman first class. Change your course north." This infuriated the captain, so he signaled back: "Dammit, I say change your course south. I'm on a battleship." To which the reply was: "And I say change your course north. I'm in a lighthouse!"

Like the captain of the battleship, we cannot afford to make assumptions about the environment. Over the past few years, to keep abreast of changes in the workplace, I've asked thousands of people in America's largest corporations about their experience of loyalty at work. As you can see in the questions and responses below, many of the employees surveyed believe that they are continuing to be loyal to organizations that are growing less loyal to them.

QUESTION 1 _____

Are you more or less loyal to your organization than you
were five years ago?

MORE (31%)   SAME (48%)   LESS (21%)

QUESTION 2 _____

Is your organization more or less loyal to you than it was
five years ago?

MORE (15%)   SAME (46%)   LESS (39%)

A *Time*/CNN poll conducted in September 1990
showed an even sharper decline in perceptions of corporate loyalty than did my study. Among the 520 workers
surveyed by Yankelovich Clancy Shulman, 57 percent said
companies are less loyal to employees today than they
were a decade ago, while 63 percent said workers are less
loyal to their firms.

NEW REALITIES _____

In the years leading to the turn of the century, organizations will face more change, complexity, and competition than they have ever faced before. To meet the
challenge of a vacillating economy and ferocious global
competition, we need to engage the spirits and creative
energies of our work force. We need their commitment and
loyalty. Yet in the last decade we have witnessed a weaken-
ing of the bonds of trust between employers and workers.

The traditional view of loyalty no longer applies.
Changes in the business world and in the work force require a different approach. Workers can no longer expect
lifetime, or even long-term, employment. Nor can they

expect stability. Change has become a fact of corporate life to be accepted and dealt with.

Employers, on the other hand, are encountering a far more mobile work force, with a different set of values than those of the previous generation. Employees today no longer believe that top management will guide their career progression. Workers are creating their own career paths, and, in many cases, consider job-hopping a normal route to professional success.

Yet opportunities abound for organizations that take the initiative in creating compelling and realistic guidelines for mutual loyalty in the workplace. But this requires a new definition of corporate loyalty and new expectations on the part of workers and management.

With traditional loyalty, everyone knew the rules: Management gave employees a sense of "family," of job security. Even if "old Joe" wasn't pulling his fair share, he could expect the company to "take care" of him by allowing him to stay in his current position or by finding him another job within the organization.

In exchange, workers gave up the right to question authority, to criticize the company, or to do their jobs in any but the "one right way" approved by the organization. They wore the company uniform, used the company product or service, and supported the organization's position on community matters. Orders were handed down the bureaucratic chain of command, followed precisely, and then released to the next level.

The new loyalty is developing around a set of expectations based on current realities. For instance, we've observed that in today's volatile business climate, organizations can no longer "parent" their employees with secure employment prospects, and more employees are job-hopping to take advantage of career opportunities at various companies.

Rather than bemoan the situation, firms like Apple

Computer stress that working at their organization will develop employees' skill and reputation, so that people will become more employable—wherever they choose to work in the future. "We'll give you five good years and you give us five good years" is not a literal part of an employment contract at Apple, but rather a philosophical acknowledgment that employment today may or may not be a long-term relationship.

THE DEFINITION OF LOYALTY

Loyalty has two dimensions: the internal or emotional level and the external, behavioral aspect. Internally, loyalty is a feeling of bonding, mutuality, affiliation, or trust. Various dictionaries define loyalty as "true, constant, or steadfast in allegiance." One definition is "faithful to a person, ideal, custom, obligation, duty or organization." Another definition is "devoted attachment and affection."

For our purposes, the key to defining loyalty starts here: *Loyalty is first of all an emotion that manifests internally as caring and concern for another person or entity. Loyalty is basic to our nature as human beings—a potent force that can be brought forth for the good of all.*

Externally, loyalty may manifest itself in a variety of ways. Since emotions are obviously invisible, it is through the behavioral dimension that we evaluate another's loyalty to us. In organizations we often have expectations of loyal behavior that are implied rather than explicit. The "loyalty contract" is an implied set of mutual expectations regarding the manifestations of loyalty by both the organization and the work force. These behaviors have changed on both sides, but many of us continue to judge loyalty by old, outdated standards. It is time for the old standards to be questioned, and for the loyalty contract to be stated openly so that employees and management can make enlightened commitments.

The mission of this book is to serve as a guide for examining and redefining ways in which loyalty is expressed in today's business environment. Twenty years ago "the company man" obeyed orders and never questioned corporate decisions. Loyal employees moved when the company said "move" and stayed when told to stay. But employees today have a different concept of loyalty. When I asked one thousand people in American corporations how they showed their loyalty, many replied that they were more willing to offer advice and criticism.

To a traditional manager who still equates loyalty with blind obedience, employee input may be interpreted as egotism or interference. To the "new style" employee, active involvement is an expression of loyalty: "I speak up because I care about what happens to this company."

"Loyalty isn't dead," says Charles Lynch, former CEO of Levolor, "it just shows up differently. Most old-school managers haven't figured that out yet."

SARA'S STORY

Flying from Washington, D.C., to San Francisco, I sat next to a highly regarded human resources specialist. Sara told me that during an interview for a management position, she had been asked a standard interview question: "Where do you see yourself with this company in ten years?"

"I don't think I made a very good impression," Sara continued. "I laughed and told them they had to be kidding—that I didn't see myself staying with any one company for the next ten years."

Nonetheless, Sara believes she is a loyal employee. According to her: "I've always chosen a company where I could be loyal to my employer. I show my loyalty by working hard, being extremely dedicated and honest, and by contributing far beyond my job description. It's just that

I'm more interested in developing my abilities than I am in staying with one organization forever."

IS LOYALTY DEAD?

When Jack Welch, chairman of General Electric, was quoted in a *Wall Street Journal* article as saying, "Loyalty to a company, it's nonsense," American management basically agreed with him. Many executives dismiss lost loyalty as the inevitable result of corporate mergers, acquisitions, and restructurings.

Frank was a loyal employee at a *Fortune* 500 company, a man on the "fast track" according to his envious peers. When the company began restructuring, Frank's career stalled. He was moved from a middle-management position into a staff function, and was finally assigned to an organizational task force.

"I never thought I'd feel this way. I used to come to work 'all fired up.' Now I simply put in my time. How am I supposed to care about what happens to the company when it doesn't care what happens to me?" Six months later Frank left to join another firm.

As surely as Frank's experience destroyed his loyalty, Samantha's loyalty was strengthened during a downsizing: "Last year we found that our entire department of thirty people was going to be eliminated. At a time of corporate-wide cutbacks, my boss relocated all of us to other jobs within the company. She really went to bat for us. She set up interviews with different department heads, checked later for feedback on how well we did, and once I even heard her on the telephone saying, 'Well, could you try him anyway? He doesn't make a very good first impression, but I promise you he can do the job.' Believe me, I am very loyal to this organization."

While some organizations strain the bonds of loyalty to the breaking point, others continue to attract and retain

valuable employees even in times of mergers and restructurings. The outcome depends in part on whether these
organizations and their employees have a realistic view of
loyalty as it manifests in changing times.

Even Mr. Welch claims to have been misquoted. In
response to the inaccuracy, he wrote to a new group of G.E.
employees: "My concept of loyalty is not 'giving time' to
some corporate entity and in turn being shielded by it
from the outside world. To me that use of the word is
'nonsense.' Loyalty is an affinity amongst people who don't
expect to be sheltered from an increasingly competitive
world; they want to grapple with it and win in it, and ask
only for fair and respectful treatment if they do not. Their
personal values and dreams and ambitions cause them to
gravitate toward each other and toward a company that
will give them the resources and the opportunity to flour-
ish and win."

WHAT'S IN IT FOR THEM?

In my national survey of one thousand employees, 95
percent of the respondents replied that they want to be
loyal. This statistic parallels another piece of research conducted in 1980 for the American Management Association.
That study concluded that although corporate loyalty had
declined among middle managers, they still wished "almost for a bonding with upper management. They wanted
to belong to something they could believe in."

In my study, the motivation for loyalty fell into three
distinct categories:

Transactional. ("I give because I get.") Some employees
want to be loyal because in their organizations loyalty is
acknowledged and rewarded. It is seen to be a determining
element in retentions, promotions, and benefits.

This is the smallest group (5 percent), and probably
reflects the decreasing number of organizations in which

employees are still promised long-term employment and a more "traditional" approach to loyalty.

Inspirational. ("I'm attracted to the organization because of what it stands for.") Other employees are inspired to be loyal by the specific mission, philosophy, or values of their organization.

A slightly larger number of people (10 percent) belong to organizations whose vision is so clear and inspiring that it attracts loyal employees who want to join and contribute to "something significant."

Integral. ("That's just the way I am.") By far, the largest number of people (85 percent) responded that they want to be loyal because it is an integral part of who they are and how they want to approach their jobs.

Loyalty is part of a deeply held desire to bond with something greater than ourselves. We were raised to be loyal: to root for local sports teams, wear our school colors, and pledge allegiance to our country. Loyalty has powerful roots in both our highest instincts and deepest beliefs.

Loyalty for most people is an inherent part of their personal work ethic. It makes work more enjoyable and fulfilling. It gives jobs meaning and importance. Perhaps most important, people feel good about themselves when they are acting loyally.

THE HIGH COST OF LOST LOYALTY _____

Lost loyalty is expensive. It is estimated to cost American business $60 billion to $70 billion annually. It has been linked to high turnover, high absenteeism, low productivity, poor quality, and increased employee theft. To fully appreciate the price your organization may be paying, you can estimate the expense incurred when replacing a valued employee: hiring, training, relocation costs, as well as the price paid in decreased production and quality while the new employee gets up to speed.

In 1988 the Bureau of National Affairs surveyed 303 companies and found that the average turnover rate was 12 percent annually. This means that a company with 1,000 employees loses an average of 120 workers each year. If the minimum cost of replacing a competent worker is 300 to 700 times that person's hourly rate (as other research suggests), then an employee making $10 per hour costs at least $3,000 to replace.

Some expenses are more difficult to quantify. What is the possible cost to your corporate reputation when disloyal employees "bad-mouth" the organization to family and friends? How might this affect other workers, potential employees, current and potential customers? How vulnerable are you to employee sabotage? Can you afford to lose corporate secrets because angry employees expose them or customer/client lists through theft? The existence of computer viruses increase the damage that can be done by disloyal individuals. A recent *Fortune* magazine article entitled "The Trust Gap" reported increased cases of employee sabotage by workers who felt they had been unfairly treated and therefore lost all loyalty to their organizations. In one example, an oil company employee erased a database worth millions of dollars, causing all drilling and exploration to be suspended worldwide until the file could be recreated.

Finally, how can you calculate the financial impact of talented employees who no longer "care about the company"—who report to work physically, but not emotionally, who hold back creative suggestions, and who reduce the amount of effort they are willing to expend on the job?

BENEFITS OF LOYALTY _____

According to surveyed employees, 93 percent said it would be in their organization's best interest to promote more loyalty. The reasons they gave are listed below:

1. Higher productivity.
2. Better work quality.
3. Higher employee morale.
4. Less turnover.
5. More employee willingness to give an "extra effort."

It is easy to apply this thinking to personal experience. Recall a time when you were working for an organization to which you had tremendous loyalty. Compare that to another work experience in which your loyalty was minimal. Answer these simple questions:

How specifically did the first company profit from your high loyalty?

What were the costs of your lower loyalty to the second company?

By comparing the list to your answers, you can see for yourself the potential for profit or loss that can be the result of just one employee's strong or weak loyalty.

LOYALTY'S CHANGING DYNAMICS _____

As a manager, you cannot afford to remain unin- formed regarding the changing dynamics of organiza- tional loyalty. To do so is to risk making costly mistakes with your work force. The issue of loyalty has traditionally been an unconscious part of employment agreements. To examine the implications of changing organizational loyalty, it is necessary to develop a conscious awareness. To begin the process, some guiding principles are useful:

LOYALTY PRINCIPLE

#1 | Loyalty begins when one party genuinely cares about another.

Loyalty starts with a sincere intent to do your best on someone else's behalf. To obtain ongoing loyalty, participants must believe that each party has a genuine concern for the well-being of the other. Jim Nordstrom is CEO of the Nordstrom chain of upscale department stores, which has gained an outstanding reputation for customer service. He says: "It's no great trick getting people to be loyal. Folks will be almost embarrassingly loyal to anyone who genuinely cares about them."

LOYALTY PRINCIPLE

#2 | For loyalty to thrive in a relationship, it must be mutual and be perceived as mutual.

Since loyalty is both an emotional state of mind and a behavior pattern, and since people judge the internal emotion by the external manifestation, your actions must be perceived to be caring by those you hope to loyalize.

Many of us have said, "Of course I love you!" to a partner who retorts, "Then why don't you act like it?" In their eyes, our behavior was not congruent with our emotions.

And many of us have been shocked to find that a valued employee left our organization because he or she felt unappreciated. "I can't believe it, I always appreciated Katherine. She should have known that." But, somehow, she did not. Again, our actions never conveyed exactly how we felt.

While it may be difficult to ascertain what behavior convinces others that we sincerely care, the effort required to do so has its rewards. The retired CEO of a chemical manufacturing company put it this way: "Loyalty is fragile. It is built or destroyed daily. At the executive level, this means that extraordinary care must be taken to keep consideration for employees a part of every corporate decision. Only then will people enthusiastically identify with the company."

LOYALTY PRINCIPLE

#3 | People have multiple loyalties that may complement or compete with one another.

People have multiple loyalties. They include personal loyalties to self and to family as well as to a professional life. Among the latter are loyalties to relationships with coworkers, subordinates, bosses, and customers. Loyalty to a person's own sense of professional standards or ethics, to career progression, to a particular project, to the department, and to the union are also important to consider when seeking loyalty to the organization.

Western Ontario University addressed this issue when reviewing their 1990 strategic plan: "We must also acknowledge and deal with the fact that inviting uncertainty, the risk of occasional failure, and a certain amount of dislocation demands that we respect the loyalty to self that a staff member must have. The institution cannot expect an individual to make great sacrifices to the university at personal expense. We will not succeed if we fail to foster an environment in which approaches to the achievement of personal and institutional goals are mutually reinforcing."

When building organizational loyalty, it is wise to position it so that it doesn't directly compete with other deeply held concerns of the work force. If loyalty to the company conflicts with other personally important loyalties, the employee may become stressed and unhappy, and his work is likely to suffer. Instead, management can find ways to "stack" multiple loyalties so that each one is seen as supportive of the others.

For example, it is not unusual these days to find employees with a heightened sense of loyalty to the customer. One technician I spoke with works for an aircraft manufacturer, making airplane "skin." His main loyalty is not to his company, his boss, or his co-workers, but rather to the future passengers of the aircraft. He has found that this loyalty is not stacked with loyalty to his employers, since he has been reprimanded many times for demanding rigid adherence to specifications.

Doubtless, this worker is viewed as a troublemaker by the organization, which has failed to understand that conflicting loyalties are at the root of the problem. Perhaps a different employer could have defused the situation by finding ways to wed the employee's sense of obligation to the customer with pride in workmanship and company loyalty.

Conflicting loyalties weaken organizational loyalty just as surely as complementary loyalties can strengthen it. Traditionally, in the Japanese culture, organizational loyalty has been stacked with other important loyalties; thus being loyal to the company is also viewed as being loyal to family, friends, co-workers, bosses, and country. (Only recently has this melding of loyalties begun to weaken, as young Japanese are starting to question the validity of old loyalties in current times.)

Managers who work with the principle of multiple loyalties help subordinates build congruent sets of loyalties. One such manager told me: "I help people find out what they are loyal to, what their personal and career goals are. Then I show them how the opportunities at this organization can best support their other loyalties."

INTO THE FUTURE

If our definition of loyalty requires the 1950s style of patriarchal companies offering lifetime job security to a work force pledging steadfast allegiance, then loyalty is indeed dead. Workers today face the reality that whether they work for a large conglomerate or a smaller entrepreneurial firm, there are no employment guarantees. Management, in turn, is dealing with a people whose values differ tremendously from those of their predecessors. Today's newer employees are educated to expect that they may work for as many as twenty different companies—in perhaps four or five different careers—over the course of their professional lives.

Stanford Research Institute's longitudinal study on the changing values of workers describes additional shifts, notably a growing number of "inner-directed" employees who care about elevating the quality of life, who want to work where they can "make a difference," and who need to be a part of "something that matters." (I will discuss the research dealing with inner-directed employees in a later section of this book.)

The death of old traditional loyalty opens opportunities for a new, enlightened form of loyalty based on shared values and goals, and mutual caring and respect. Organizations can benefit by tapping into the commitment of their workers. Employees yearn to feel emotionally connected to their work. It is the right time to address these mutual needs and to redefine loyalty in ways that will serve both. ⌐

Assessing the Loyalty Factor _____

I've asked hundreds of managers to answer a series of questions from the point of view of their subordinates. After their work force fills out the same questionnaire, we compare the two sets of answers. Almost always, management is surprised by the responses of their employees.

Try this yourself. Answer these questions the way you believe your subordinates will. Then ask them to fill out the same questionnaire. Compare the results.

1. Are you more or less loyal to your organization than you were five years ago? MORE LESS SAME

2. Is your organization more or less loyal to you than it was five years ago? MORE LESS SAME

3. What do you specifically do to show your loyalty?

4. Is it to your advantage to be loyal? Why?

5. Would it be in your organization's best interest to promote more loyalty? Why?

6. What do you specifically want management to do to better demonstrate its loyalty to you?

7. What does management currently do that demonstrates its loyalty to you?

8. Does being loyal to the organization conflict with any of your other loyalties? How?

Unless you have assessed the loyalty factor from your subordinates' perspective, you may also be making some erroneous assumptions.

While this book can act as a general guideline for management practices and policies which loyalize, your own work force remains your best source of information.

WHY BOTHER?

"Loyalty is all there is." "I've always had to work where I could be one hundred percent loyal." "If given the choice between a group of people who are highly skilled but have low loyalty, and one with average skills and high loyalty—I'd pick the loyal group because I know that somehow they'd make it happen."

Opinions like these, gathered from thousands of people across the United States, demonstrate that loyalty is a key ingredient in the employee/management relationship.

In the rest of the book we will look at loyalty from the employees' perspective, explore management practices that loyalize subordinates, and examine the ways in which organizations can develop loyalty through corporate policies and procedures.

2 | THE EMPLOYEES' AGENDA

THE CROQUET GAME

Alice thought she had never seen such a curious croquet-ground in her life: it was all ridges and furrows; the croquet-balls were live hedgehogs, and the mallets live flamingoes, and the soldiers had to double themselves up and stand on their hands and feet, to make the arches.

The chief difficulty Alice found at first was in managing her flamingo: she succeeded in getting his body tucked away, comfortably enough, under her arm, with its legs hanging down, but generally, just as she had got its neck nicely straightened out, and was going to give the hedgehog a blow with its head, it *would* twist itself round and look up into her face, with such a puzzled expression that she could not help bursting out laughing: and when she had got its head down, and was going to begin again, it was very provoking to find that the hedgehog had unrolled itself, and was in the act of crawling away: besides all this, there was generally a ridge or a furrow in the way wherever she wanted to send the hedgehog to, and, as the doubled-up soldiers were always getting up and walking off to other parts of the ground, Alice soon came to the conclusion that it was a very difficult game indeed.

The players all played at once without waiting for turns, quarrelling all the while, and fighting for the hedgehogs, and in a very short time the Queen was in a furious passion, and went stamping about and shouting, "Off with his head!" or "Off with her head!" about once in a minute.

Alice began to feel very uneasy: to be sure, she had not as yet had any dispute with the Queen, but she knew that it might happen at any minute, "and then," thought she, "what would become of me? They're dreadfully fond of beheading people here; the great wonder is, that there's anyone left alive!"

—Lewis Carroll, *Alice in Wonderland*

WORKERS IN WONDERLAND

Like Lewis Carroll's Alice, employees today struggle to make sense of a world turned upside down. If they've been in the work force for over five years, their companies are operating differently than the way they did when these workers first signed up—structure, position in the marketplace, function, mission, even the company name and ownership may have changed. Their jobs have been altered since they first accepted them, and skills they spent years developing may now be obsolete. The rules have been changed so often, they aren't even sure which "game" they're playing.

And this is only the beginning. Futurists forecast continuing organizational restructuring, change, and uncertainty. In fact, it is predicted that the forces of global competition, the increase of mergers and buyouts, and the explosion of advances in technology will drive organizations to respond at increasingly accelerated rates.

THE NEW GUIDING VALUES

As powerful as these outside forces are, they pale in comparison to changes going on within the hearts and minds of the American worker. While external influences confront them, employees are also experiencing an internal values shift.

The term *values* describes the attitudes, beliefs, opinions, hopes, fears, prejudices, needs, desires, and aspirations that, taken together, govern how one behaves. One's interior set of values finds holistic expression in a lifestyle.

The values and lifestyles (VALS) typography developed by Stanford Research Institute International (SRI) is one attempt to analyze the lives of Americans to discover why people believe and act as they do. The typography is composed of four major groups, each with subgroups. *Need-driven* people are characterized by poverty and struggle to meet their own basic needs. *Integrateds,* on the other hand, are financially comfortable; they have developed an open, self-assured, self-expressive outlook on life and are possessed of a global perspective. For our purposes, two other groups—the *outer-directeds* and *inner-directeds*—will be discussed in depth. Members of these two groups make up the largest segment of the population. The inner-directed group, as we will see, is the fastest growing.

Outer-directeds

This group makes up "middle America" and is by far the largest. The majority of the work force is currently composed of outer-directed employees. The subgroups are *belongers, emulators,* and *achievers.*

Belongers are traditional, conservative, family-oriented, and patriotic. Their key drive is to fit in, not to stand out.

Emulators are ambitious, competitive, and hard-working people who push themselves to achieve and succeed.

Achievers are those Americans who built "the system" and are now at its helm. They are a diverse group of self-reliant and highly successful people.

Inner-directeds

This population segment is the only one expected to increase in the 1990s. Currently 28 percent of the work force, its numbers are highest in California, where one-half of the employee base is composed of people who are inner-directed.

*"I-Am-Me"*s are the youngest members in VALS categories, with an average age of twenty-one. These Americans are in a tumultuous transition from the outer-directed perspective with which they were raised to an inner-directed way of thinking, which involves a discovery of new interests and a setting of new life goals.

Experimentals are generally older than the "I-Am-Me"s, and have removed themselves further from the outer-directed lifestyles in which they were also brought up. They seek direct, vivid experience. They are well educated and hold high-paying technical and professional jobs.

Socially conscious are those people whose primary concerns encompass societal issues, trends, and events. They are successful, influential, and mature.

MARRIOTT AND HYATT

A few years ago, SRI used these data to analyze the ongoing advertising campaigns of archrivals Marriott Corporation and Hyatt Corporation, both of which promote their hotels to upper-income business professionals.

In their magazine ads Marriott tended to emphasize luxury, by showing their guests arriving in a Rolls-Royce, while the Hyatt's ad campaigns boasted of serving herbal tea and other natural foods in their restaurant. Probably without realizing it, Marriott was appealing to the outer-directed, while Hyatt appealed to a more inner-directed customer. In SRI's view, Hyatt may fare better in the end because of the expected growth of the inner-directed group.

INNER-DIRECTEDS ON THE JOB _____

Today's newer employees are likely to belong to this increasingly influential group of inner-driven people. Their needs will compel organizations to consider a new business ethic.

INNER-DIRECTED EMPLOYEE PROFILE

1. They want to be able to say, "I am a good person."
2. They want jobs that are personally satisfying and rewarding.
3. They care about quality-of-life and personal growth issues.
4. They want to be part of "something that matters."
5. They feel they have a right to fair and honest treatment.
6. They want control over the decisions affecting their lives.
7. They want to be loyal and to identify with the values and policies of their organizations.

Individualistic and independent, today's talented "gold collar" workers (as SRI has dubbed them) also know they are important to their companies. A computer programmer in the middle of a project can't be easily replaced. And they demand to be treated with respect, to have their importance acknowledged by the organization.

THE ROLE OF EMOTION IN BUSINESS _____

In his recent book, *Passions Within Reason: The Strategic Role of Emotions,* Cornell University professor Robert H. Frank states that emotions are not just the "fuzzy thinking" that most other economists believe them to be. Rather, he says, emotions serve a highly useful function. They short-circuit some types of self-interested behavior by bonding people to external projects, to beliefs, and to relationships which are not always in the individual's narrow self-interest. Emotions cause people to feel strongly about things outside themselves.

Loyalty is an emotional state. While it benefits management to address the issue of loyalty, the corporate world has historically ignored emotional issues for a variety of reasons. As I've suggested, many people dismiss emotions as unreal or as "fuzzy thinking." Others understand that emotions are real but feel they have no place in business. Still others understand that emotions might be used to build motivation and commitment to an organizational enterprise, but don't know how to go about achieving this. Understanding more about the makeup of inner-directed individuals is a good beginning.

To the growing group of inner-directed employees, emotions are a real and essential part of doing business. They value and trust their feelings. They are seeking a quality of worklife that includes deeply personal satisfactions: they want to love their work and bond emotionally with their organization. Tapping the full potential of this kind of worker will go beyond engaging their physical energies and intellectual capacities; it will also require touching their hearts.

Their desire to make worthwhile contributions is so strong that 80 percent of the 1988 graduating class of Harvard M.B.A.'s said they didn't want to work for any large company. They felt that none of the *Fortune* 500 organizations offered the individual a chance to be of value and to really make a difference.

Utilizing the concepts of outer- and inner-directed individuals can be useful in preparing for a trend which will witness greater numbers of people in search of self-fulfillment. Inner-directed individuals are more in touch with their emotions and expect employment to satisfy certain emotional needs.

THE SEARCH FOR MEANING

Flotation tanks, brain-wave biofeedback, subliminal suggestion tapes that "program" the brain with more productive thought modes—these terms are creeping into the vocabulary of otherwise normal people. And some enterprises are already capitalizing on people's demand for New Age thinking and values.

- A software company markets a package that allows users to customize subliminal messages onto their computer screens.

- In Los Angeles, the Altered States Flotation Center and Mind Gym draws its clients from the mainstream—lawyers, managers, secretaries, Japanese businessmen.

- Omega's new "Symbol" collection—luxury timepieces priced as high as $19,000—are decorated with yin-yang symbols and astrological signs.

- Training experts are remarking on the growing demand for such New Age training regimens as fire-walking and self-hypnosis.

- Hanna-Barbera grossed $20 million for the first two years of their Bible videocassette series.

People are searching for deeper meaning. Whether they are meditating on crystals, practicing Buddhist

chants, or reading conventional Bible stories, today's New
Age thinkers and spiritual seekers are a growing segment
of the work force.

New Agers represent the most affluent, well-educated,
successful segment of the baby boom. What was once considered occult thinking is now mainstream. According to
the National Opinion Research Council of the University of
Chicago, two-thirds of Americans have had a psychic experience, and 42 percent say they have had contact with the
dead.

I was reminded of how much times have changed in
this respect when I was attending a conference last year.
The speaker suggested to the audience that we are not
human beings having a spiritual experience, but rather
spiritual beings having a human experience. This is a mes-
sage which has been expressed before by religious teach-
ers, philosophers, and even a few quantum physicists. The
difference here was the audience. Our speaker was addressing two thousand real-estate employees at a national
sales meeting.

THE WHOLE-LIFE TRACK

Flying home from the East Coast, I sat next to an
executive who handed me his business card. I was startled
when he abruptly snatched it back. He explained that he
wanted to cross out the word *senior* in front of his vice-
presidential title.

He went on to tell me that he was only temporarily
acting in the senior position and that, as soon as possible,
he wanted to get back to his old job. He said that five years
ago his ambition was to be the president of the company,
but not anymore: "Being a vice president suits me just
fine. I'm good at it, and I could do it in my sleep. Who
needs all the hassle and pressure of a higher position?

Besides, I've got a couple of entrepreneurial ventures going, and this gives me all the time I need to 'play' with them."

Increasingly, people are looking to balance a variety of interests and loyalties. They are not as likely to think, as do some of their bosses, that the world begins and ends with the office or factory. In my study, this idea was expressed in a variety of ways:

- "I like my job, but I have a lot of interests outside the office."
- "I would put several things ahead of the organization."
- "I love my job, but it's not my whole life."
- "If the company decided to relocate, I wouldn't go along. I like my lifestyle too much."

Proposed in an article for the *Harvard Business Review*, the "mommy track"—or slower track—was envisioned as an option that employers should offer all women. In return for more flexible work hours, women with families could choose a career track with fewer opportunities for advancement.

A poll of seven hundred residents in Northern California found that a whopping 90 percent would go even further, and agreed that employers should offer a two-track career path to everyone—male or female.

Among the significant findings:

- 62 percent of the women polled would choose the mommy track, and only a third would opt for more promotions over flexible work hours.
- Among men, 47 percent would choose a daddy track. Two in five men—42 percent—would prefer chances for promotions.

A similar study by Robert Half International produced even more startling results. According to their poll, the parent track was preferred by 82 percent of the females and 74 percent of the males. Over half of the men in this study said they would give up 25 percent of their salaries for more personal or family time.

There are many reasons why people would prefer a career progression that is other than traditional. Some want to spend more time with their families while others have side businesses or hobbies that require much of their attention and energy. Still others find that promotions bring personal penalties.

An employee at a utilities company was thirty pounds overweight. He complained to me that he once had his weight under control. In fact, his whole life used to be better. In the past, he enjoyed his work as a laborer and did it well. His friends were fellow employees who joined him after work to play sports and to exercise.

His problems started when his company promoted him to supervisor. As a result, he no longer did the physical labor he enjoyed. He no longer worked with his buddies. Instead, he traveled by car all day checking on various sites. His hours changed, and he lost social contact with his friends. He quit exercising ("It's no fun alone"). He hated his job and he was miserable.

When I asked him why he didn't request a return to his former work, he said he could never do that. The company wouldn't understand somebody not wanting a promotion; he believed they would probably fire him.

Despite potential damage to careers, some professionals still opt for nontraditional alternatives. An association executive announced she would not renew her annual contract. She and her husband were going to take a one-year "sabbatical" traveling through Europe. "You have to make a choice between keeping on the fast track or taking time out for other parts of your life. We've both been listening to our inner voices for a long time. We are following our bliss."

THE MANAGER AS AN EMPLOYEE

As a manager, you are first of all an employee of your organization. You have your own issues of loyalty to address before you can help loyalize others. Eleanor Roosevelt once said, "No one can make you feel inferior without your consent." In the same vein, no one can make you feel loyal without your consent. Loyalty is not just a top-down process. There are several ways that all employees can participate in developing loyalty, once they have decided to do so. Here are a variety of suggestions given to me by management employees:

1. Find something you love to do. Tommy Lasorda, manager of the Los Angeles Dodgers, says loyalty comes easily when you really love what you're doing. It is easy to be loyal to an organization which gives you the chance to do work you consider challenging and exciting.

2. Seek an organization that mirrors your own philosophy and ethical standards. During preemployment interviews, ask about company values and principles. (What is their mission? How do they treat people? What do they value when making decisions or setting priorities?)

   One loyal manager told me: "The thing I like best about working here is that this organization does business fairly. I'm comfortable with their ethics. They reflect my own."

3. Know what your goals and priorities are. Take stock of your personal and professional objectives. In light of your own goals, what are the unique opportunities offered by this organization? Get a sense of which things are most important in your life and which are negotia-

ble. We all have multiple loyalties, but each is not necessarily valued equally. Knowing ahead of time what your
priorities are will help you choose wisely when investing time and emotion in a project.

4. Educate yourself to the benefits provided by your organization. One national bank has a very generous benefits
   package with exceptionally good maternity policies. A
   female manager said she didn't realize that the program they offered was special until she participated on
   a committee which compared other companies' benefits. She remarked: "I am very impressed with the concern and sensitivity this organization shows me."

5. Develop a realistic perspective of today's business environment. You may yearn for a simpler, more secure
   work environment, but you need to accept the fact that
   times have changed. Today, companies are bought and
   sold like baseball cards traded on a back-street lot. One
   day your industry is regulated, the next day it's not. Just
   when you think you've got your job figured out, the
   business climate changes again. That's the new reality!

6. Seek stimulating challenges at work. Stay on the look-
   out for projects that interest and stimulate you. You
   cannot afford to wait for the organization to create your
   career path. You can keep yourself challenged.

   • Develop a checklist of skills and personal qualities
     required for your current position. Then rate your
     abilities in all necessary areas, and set up a long-
     range self-development program.

   • Request lateral moves that expose you to different
     departments and functions, and thus broaden your
     background and experiences. Ask different depart-
     ment heads within the company about their manage-
     ment needs and criteria.

   • Volunteer for task forces or committees, especially
     those involving many different levels and points of
     view. Socialize with a variety of people at work.

first of all it takes a willingness to evaluate your own actions through the eyes of your employees.

THE EYE OF THE BEHOLDER

TEETOTALER: "If I pour water on a plant, it grows and thrives. If I pour liquor on the same plant, it shrivels up and dies. Now what does that show you?"

DRINKER: "If you want to grow a plant in your stomach, drink water."

The humor in this joke pivots on our understanding that two people can view the same phenomenon and come to different conclusions about its meaning.

In sales, knowing what will convince a particular customer is crucial to success, as the following story illustrates:

An insurance salesman stuck his head into a sales manager's office door and said, "You don't want to buy any insurance, do you?"

"Young man, whoever taught you to sell? You never say, 'You don't want to buy insurance, do you?'" The sales manager continued to lecture the young man on salesmanship, stressing that every customer's needs are different. "What you lack is confidence. I'll buy some of your insurance to give you confidence."

The appropriate papers were signed. "Now remember what I told you. Every customer is different. You must use different approaches for each customer." "Oh, I do that already," said the salesman. "This is my approach for sales managers, and it works almost every time."

THE PLATINUM RULE

One's perception of an event, rather than the event itself, defines one's reality. My intention means nothing, for

• Sign up for interesting company-sponsored training and seminars. Take advantage of all that the organization has to offer.

7. Show your appreciation. Stay aware of the various ways in which your company shows its loyalty to you. Whenever your organization does something that demonstrates its respect or caring, let top management know that you noticed. Send a note to your direct boss or to the executive suite, write a "point-of-view" article for the in-house magazine, or post a thank-you card on the company billboard.

   One sales manager read an article about his company's refusal to deal with any country where "under the table" money was part of the negotiation process. He circled the article, wrote the words *right on* in the column, and mailed it to his CEO.

8. Plan to leave the organization. In today's business environment, restructurings are a way of life. Layoffs that have no bearing on performance or qualifications occur routinely. The wise employee freely gives loyalty to professional relationships knowing they may or may not be permanent.

   Even ex-employees can remain loyal to their former employers. They continue to speak well of the firm, become consumers of the company's product or service, and may even return to employment or act as a consultant to the organization. Bonds of loyalty can continue to serve both parties long after the original relationship has ended.

3 | MANAGING FOR LOYALTY

People want to be involved at work, but they are
tain if they can commit and trust.

People want to contribute their creative efforts, bu
don't know if it's safe to take the risk.

People want to be loyal, but they don't want their
to go unreciprocated.

People want visionary, trustworthy leaders wh
explain the new realities and inspire commitment
organization's success. This kind of leadership is no
the exclusive preserve of the inhabitants occupy
corporate tower. An executive, a manager, a sup
even an hourly employee can learn to develop a v
the future, to inspire others, and to build trust and
among subordinates and peers.

This new way of thinking is spreading across
Even when loyalty is not part of the corporate pol
are individual managers—especially the inner-d
who are changing things at their own levels.

Managing for loyalty from any corporate
quires knowledge, sensitivity, and skill. It also ne
a congruent and consistent set of values and po

instance, if I can't convey it in ways which you understand and agree with.

People "buy in" for different reasons. That is why in management, the Golden Rule ("Do unto others as you would have others do unto you") is sometimes not enough. When we treat others as we would like to be treated, we take it for granted that they are just like us. When we try to convince others with evidence that is conclusive for us, we are assuming that the same arguments are convincing to everyone. When we show employees concern, respect, and caring in ways we would choose to have these feelings shown to us, we may only be understood by a work force of clones.

It is far more effective to sell, convince, or manage according to the Platinum Rule, which states:

> Do unto others as they would
> have you do unto them.

Today's work force is scared, scarred, and skeptical. They are wisely withholding their full emotional investment until they see a demonstration of loyalty from management. Before they care once again about their companies, they want to be sure their companies care about them. As AFL-CIO president Lane Kirkland succinctly stated: "Never love a company that can't love you back."

One thousand employees suggested five areas where they needed to see management improve. Respondents said they were most convinced of management's genuine concern about employees when there was a display of:

1. Honest communication.

2. Recognition and appreciation.

3. Employee participation in decisions.

4. Professional and personal development.

5. Equitable salaries and benefits.

Some bosses inspire loyalty, while others make it difficult for even the most loyal employee to feel connected to the company.

When the renowned Broadway director and choreographer Bob Fosse died, reporters commented on the immense loyalty the performers showed him. One dancer summed it up for everyone when she said: "We always knew that whatever Bob asked us to do—even if it was difficult or felt awkward—was to make us look good."

An executive I spoke with said practically the same thing about his best bosses: "The one thing they all had in common was a sincere desire to see others succeed."

Are your intentions that clear? Do your employees know that you want them to look good, to excel, to be successful?

ACTIONS THAT KILL LOYALTY

When managers—even well-meaning ones—disregard the needs and expectations of their subordinates, they can behave in ways that reduce loyalty.

Of course, the cartoons that follow are an exaggeration—or at least they're meant to be. But if you answer "yes" to any of the questions, try and remember how it affected your feelings about yourself, your boss, and your company. Probably it was a lose–lose–lose situation.

Have you reported to someone who discouraged employee input and participation?

Have you worked for a boss who took sole credit for the efforts of an entire team?

Have you ever had a manager who was less than candid?

Have you been asked to make a major change without proper training?

Have you ever worked where salary and benefits were obviously inequitable?

Communicate for Loyalty _____

In a study of hundreds of workers, management professor Jim Kouzes asked: "What traits do you look for in a supervisor?"

With incredible consistency, respondents gave first preference to honesty. It was no coincidence that I also found openness and honesty to be reiterated as essential ingredients for developing loyalty between managers and workers.

When a vice president took over a new department, she met with her staff. "I can keep you informed in either of two ways. I can let you know what is happening as soon as I know anything definite, or I can keep you informed of everything I learn—but you have to remember, some of this information will be sketchy, half-formed, and sometimes not totally accurate."

Unanimously, her staff chose the second option.

Employees feel, with good reason, that their lives are affected by many occurrences over which they have no control. A merger may be pending; the company could be moving; the whole department might be closing down. An air of secrecy adds fuel to the uncertainty.

There will always be times when you are not at liberty to discuss what you know with subordinates. When you don't know all the details yourself, it is best to make this clear rather than being trapped with the appearance of deceit. It is more acceptable to employees to hear from you that you cannot divulge information than to be told "I don't know" when they have reason to suspect that you do.

In times of crisis, word should come down from the top. Salomon Brothers' plan to close down its municipal finance department was leaked to the press on a Friday. The *New York Times* printed the story on Saturday. Chairman John Gutfreund wasted no time in calling a mass meeting on the trading floor first thing Monday morning. That meeting clearly had a calming effect, especially when

those who were departing realized what magnificent sever-
ance packages they'd be taking with them. The morale-
boosting to those remaining was "We'll be shrinking a
little bit, but don't you worry, we're not trying to hide
anything from you and we'll still treat you well."

It means a great deal to the person who has to stand
up there and represent the organization if the company
has fostered positive feelings among its employees—if
there has been a history of candid communication from
those in management.

A difficult role was thrust upon Ken Bertaccini, a vice
president with AT&T. In the mid-1980s, he was given sixteen thousand employees with the task of reducing them
by half. He was to be responsible for terminating eight
thousand employees—the largest single cut in personnel in
the entire history of the company.

Ken gathered large employee groups and told them
the news in person. He reported the reasons for the layoffs
and the ways in which they would be determined. He
outlined the "profile" of those most likely to be cut, how
those laid off would be treated, and the ways in which
those that remained would be handled.

When he finished one of these grueling deliveries, a
man approached him onstage. This twenty-year veteran of
the company knew his job was in peril. Tears were stream-
ing down his cheeks, but as he got to Ken, he said: "Thank
you for treating me like an adult."

Candor is not just for times of crisis or upheaval. In
order to develop trust, it is absolutely essential that subordinates know they can rely on management for honest
information as well as personal performance appraisal.
When a manager shares his or her understanding of the
organization's goals, and feedback on job performance as
it relates to those goals, employees develop a longer-range
view of the company and their place in it.

Employees need honest information even before they

are hired. It is important to accurately portray job requirements—both the positive and the negative aspects—to the
candidate. An equally candid description of the organization's culture will help a prospective employee hold realistic expectations, and will increase the likelihood that the
person will feel satisfied once on the job.

A critical factor in developing commitment is employee belief in management's effectiveness. Employees
who think that management is doing a good job of running
the organization are more likely to identify with organizational goals. Research shows that this belief is heavily
influenced by the dependability and credibility of management's communication practices.

Clearly, effective communication channels are vital for
building employee loyalty. People want timely information
that explains a course of action and why particular decisions are made. They want to know how decisions fit the
corporate mission and objectives, and exactly how new
policies affect the way they do their job. They expect ongoing elaboration on the ways in which their job or function
contributes to the goals of the organization.

To build skills at communicating for loyalty, compare
your current practices with those listed. How many are
already a part of your management style?

1. Use employee opinion surveys and announce the results.

2. Provide accurate expectations and feedback.

3. Explain the reasons behind decisions and policies.

4. Be absolutely candid at all times.

5. Explain how individual contributions support the
   goals of the company.

6. Explain specifically how individual jobs are changed
   by decisions.

7. Let people know what the organization stands for—its mission, philosophy, values.

8. Let people know what you stand for—your ethics, philosophy, values.

9. Time your communications so that there are no "surprises."

10. Hold exit interviews.

Developing strong communication skills can be difficult. It takes time and patience to send clear messages and to insure they are understood. And it's not always easy to be candid. Keeping secrets can be a way of trying to manipulate events or people. Often managers equate knowledge with power and are reluctant to share information and give up their control. A manager under pressure to produce results may have to guard against slipping into these unproductive modes of behavior. The effort is worthwhile.

When bosses can't—or won't—share necessary information, anxieties and resentments build in their people. One seasoned manager I spoke with, kept in the dark by his vice president about the purpose and extent of a major cutback in his department, took a couple of star performers with him when he left.

An important, but often overlooked, component of communication is nonverbal behavior. Managers who play power games by seating a visitor in a lower chair, ignoring people for a few minutes as they enter the office, or keeping employees waiting past an agreed meeting time communicate loud and clear that they are manipulators. Whatever else is "said" in the subsequent meeting will be filtered through this nonverbal statement.

Communicating for trust and loyalty requires a special sensitivity to nonverbal skills. UCLA, in a classic piece of research, found that what people believe when you tell them something depends 7 percent on the content, 38 percent on your tone of voice, and 55 percent on how you look. If the words you speak are not congruent with the way that you say them—or with your facial expression, body stance, and gestures, for example—you will not be believed.

The great communicators in management today are not necessarily the finest orators. Instead, they are the people whom we automatically trust, whose sincerity is reflected in their verbal and nonverbal communications, and who "walk their talk."

RECOGNIZE AND SHOW APPRECIATION _____

The days are gone when an annual "gesture" of recognition—the company picnic or awards dinner—can overshadow callous treatment by management during the rest of the year. One unhappy employee put it this way: "How stupid do they think we are? Do they really believe that a lousy chicken dinner is going to make up for treating us like robots?"

When employees today speak of recognition and appreciation, they're talking about an ongoing acknowledgment of their contribution to the organization. They are looking for respect, trust, and personal attention. Managers validate these needs when they:

1. *Interact with personnel at the human level.* This means showing concern for employees not only professionally but also personally. One management executive, who is especially good at loyalizing people, likes to ask others what aspect of the company they manage. He gets answers like "data processing," "the office staff," or "the human resources department." Then he tells them that he manages weddings, divorces, pregnancies, and family crises—all the "human" conditions.

From time to time, employees have personal problems. The boss who responds with compassion and support demonstrates loyalty in a way that subordinates understand and appreciate.

Employees are individuals who are motivated in different ways. By staying sensitive to people's uniqueness, you can tailor rewards to match their recipients. A boss I know acknowledged the good work of a married female employee by sending two letters of appreciation—one to her and one to her husband. The employee felt doubly rewarded.

To get to know employees as individuals, spend some time together away from the office. Rapport develops as people discover things they have in common. (A saleswoman was terrified of her "perfect" boss until they went to lunch together. When her manager got spinach stuck between her teeth, the saleswoman relaxed completely.)

When areas of disagreement are also uncovered, treat them as strengths for better problem-solving. As a wise manager once said: "If you and I are in a meeting and we both agree, one of us is redundant."

Managers who show public appreciation for their employees don't care if it appears "hokey" to outsiders. This Thanksgiving, as last, Allen Paulson, CEO of Gulfstream Aerospace, will don a chef's hat and serve turkey to employees, wishing each one well by name. Thomas Melohn, CEO of North American Tool and Die, awards a "Super Person of the Month" plaque which is prominently and permanently displayed in the plant. Herb Kelleher, CEO of Southwest Air, sends out thousands of personalized valentines each Valentine's Day.

2. *Show people how their efforts matter.* When Ford Motor Company created the Taurus automobile, they took a prototype on tour to the various parts suppliers. By doing this, they showed exactly how those suppliers' products contributed to the finished product. The response was overwhelming. Employees from each company wrote un-

solicited letters pledging to continue their best efforts on behalf of Ford.

Everyone benefits when people know the value of their work. A television director who has been employed by CBS for over twenty-five years said: "There are two ways to 'pull' performance from a cast and crew. One is to intimidate them. The other is to put your ego aside and make them as big a part of the overall success as possible. The second way works better."

You can begin by making your praise more explicit. Instead of saying, "You did a good job," try stating it more like this: "You handled that last customer very well. When she became upset, you stayed relaxed and helpful. That is exactly the kind of service our organization stands for."

3. *Treat people with dignity and respect.* Trust, respect, and consistency in relationships have always been important to business success. These traits, however, take on added significance today. Managers can model the kinds of loyal behaviors they expect from their subordinates.

- Listen to people.
- Set clear expectations.
- Delegate responsibility and authority.
- Keep all your explicit and implicit promises.
- Acknowledge success publicly and offer negative feedback only in private.
- Encourage questions.
- Give people control over as much as possible.

Managers develop loyal employees by being loyal bosses. This is reflected by many managers I've interviewed: "My people always come first." "You get loyalty by giving it." "If I go all out for them, they will go all out for the company."

One manager told an employee that she would back him to the end. If he chose to resign over an unfair company policy, she'd resign with him. "I think that did it. The employee didn't want me to jeopardize my career, so he dropped the whole issue."

4. *Provide an enjoyable place for people to work.* Employees who were most loyal to their organizations talked about them as "fun" places to work. Some managers create an enjoyable atmosphere and people look forward to coming to work.

- On Fridays, in a small West Coast manufacturing company, employees pass around the "joke of the week." "It's just our way of keeping things in perspective," the manager said. "After all, we're not curing cancer."

- One office manager locates photographs of famous people and puts them on the bulletin board with a make-believe greeting from the celebrity to the staff for their fine work. It is always timely and funny.

- Dryers Ice Cream Company has "free ice cream day" for employees every Wednesday.

- At North American Tool and Die, every payday the owners buy donuts for the entire plant.

On April Fool's Day a few years ago, Scott McNealy, the founder and CEO of Sun Microsystems, found his office transformed into a miniature golf course. The night before, employees had torn out the wall behind McNealy's desk, removed the furniture, and covered the floor with fresh sod and miniature sand traps.

Such outrageous stunts are not only tolerated by Sun's exuberant leader, they are savored. Says McNealy: "We're trying hard to be different from other companies. One of our goals is to provide an environment that people have a blast working in."

University National Bank and Trust in California is famous for two things: outstanding customer service and a sense of humor and fun. On the side of the bank building is a mural of a Martian leaving its spacecraft. Newspaper adds are humorous. Once a year, the CEO offers bags of Walla-Walla onions to all customers.

At UNB there is no personnel department, yet they hire the best talent in the industry. Says one happily employed vice president: "The banking business is a small world. We know one another's reputations. And everyone who works here has a list of professional acquaintances who want to join us because we pay well and because it sounds like fun."

Robert Paluck, the CEO of Convex Computer, enlivened the annual company picnic by sliding into seventy-two gallons of iced raspberry Jell-O. Five vice presidents followed him into the goo. Paluck believes these kinds of special events give his company a competitive edge by inspiring enthusiasm among his employees.

It also sounds like fun at Ben and Jerry's Homemade, Inc. Jerry Greenfield (one of the founders of the gourmet ice cream company in Vermont) formed a committee that initiated free massages, created an Elvis day, and sponsored a Halloween costume contest.

Managers at all levels endear themselves to employees when they help people "lighten up" and have fun while they work. Sometimes the rewards that make the most lasting impressions are the small, "silly" things—the bouquet of balloons, the funny thank-you card, the singing telegram, or the award "roast."

5. *Notice the importance of details.* Little things can mean a lot when it comes to job satisfaction. In times of uncertainty, details take on great symbolic significance. People begin dwelling on small inconveniences—malfunctioning copy machines, potholes in the parking lot, rips in the carpet, empty paper towel dispensers in the

bathroom—whenever overall faith in management is shaky.

Management's attention to detail in the physical work environment gives people a feeling of confidence. On the other hand, employees may sense that their organization is wrestling with even larger problems if it can't meet the most basic needs of the work force. People may suppose, for example, that the company is tightening its belt because of poor profits. In any case, inattentiveness to the small things is sure to send the wrong signal.

6. *Expect subordinates to be trustworthy, committed, and loyal.* The powerful influence of one person's expectation on another's behavior is known as the Pygmalion Effect. Eliza Doolittle explains it in George Bernard Shaw's play *Pygmalion:* "You see, really and truly, apart from the things anyone can pick up, the difference between a lady and a flower girl is not how she behaves but how she's treated. I shall always be a flower girl to Professor Higgins because he always treats me as a flower girl and always will; but I know I can be a lady to you because you always treat me as a lady and always will."

The difference between managers who "just can't find good people today" and those who speak with pride of the hard work and dedication of their employees may be a direct result of their attitudes toward subordinates.

FOSTER PARTICIPATION

Many of America's managers build employee loyalty by encouraging active participation in decision-making. One such CEO told me: "We communicate with our people like crazy. Quarterly our employees tell us what to do."

It is not always a simple process. Gathering and properly responding to employee input means more than putting up a suggestion box. It means coaching employees on how to make suggestions, how to go beyond pointing out flaws to offering constructive advice. Employees need to know what kind of suggestions are useful as well as those which are not. They need to be exposed to the criteria that upper management uses when evaluating ideas. All employees should be educated in basic creative problem-solving skills.

Beyond that, managers increase participation when they:

Ask for suggestions upfront. Employees feel they can have some impact if they are asked to contribute ideas before a decision is made.

Respond to suggestions. Evaluating ideas in open meetings helps employees see their input in the context of company goals and objectives. It is particularly important that the employee knows why an idea was rejected, or how it could be altered to better fit the company's overall strategy.

Encourage curiosity. Curiosity is the vanguard of creativity. People are constantly exposed to innovative ideas in the daily media, industry journals, and during conversations with other professionals. When employees are encouraged to be curious, to look and listen for new ideas, they begin to notice innovations everywhere—where they dine out, get their hair cut, or go to an exercise class.

Allow mistakes and failures. Linus Pauling once said that the way to have a few good ideas is to have lots of ideas. Most of those ideas will be "wrong"—that is, not the best choice for this particular application at this point in time. Wrong ideas, mistakes, and failures are all part of the game.

Adopt useful suggestions. People lose enthusiasm when their participation has little or no effect on how the organization is run. Employees are encouraged when they see their ideas incorporated into company policies.

Build participative teams. Create teams and cross-group task forces to blend a diversity of ideas and approaches to problem-solving. Take people off-site, to retreat facilities that encourage informality. Let employees get to know one another before you ask them to function as a team. Teach everyone the steps to productive brainstorming sessions.

There are several tools on the market to help managers develop employees into creative problem-solving teams. *Creativity in Business*, a book I authored, is a compilation of basic creative-thinking techniques—idea generation, mind-mapping, metaphorical thinking, brainstorming—that can be used for teaching creativity and innovation.

The best instrument that I've found to enhance team-building is the *InQ Questionnaire*. This self-assessment questionnaire provides a model of participants' style of thinking—synthesist, idealist, pragmatist, analyst, or realist. Not only do people get a better understanding of their own thinking preferences, they discover the value of other styles being represented in their teams for well-rounded problem-solving sessions.

Having presented workshops using the InQ with sales and management groups in a variety of organizations, I have always found it effective for fostering productive teams.

Recognize and reward contributors. Give full credit to those whose suggestions are adopted. Publicize their efforts, give them a share of the additional revenue (or savings) generated by their ideas, and make them organizational heroes.

All of this pays off well for the manager who is seen as approachable and available, and who takes the time to make participation work. The creative input of your employees can advance the entire department.

One bank president told me: "Our employee loyalty has greatly improved as we've included more people in the decision-making process and allowed them to develop pride in their contribution to our overall success."

Develop a sense of responsibility and capability in

your employees and it will build into loyalty and commitment. Encourage them to participate and they will excel.
Get them to think of the company as their own and they
will express their loyalty by speaking up. Let them know
that their participation is a valued addition, rather than a
personal risk, and employees will go to great lengths to
contribute.

PROMOTE PROFESSIONAL AND PERSONAL DEVELOPMENT ____

Employees who feel good about their jobs are more
loyal. A job that involves a high degree of autonomy, offers
a wide variety of tasks, and challenges an employee to
stretch professionally toward a meaningful goal will enhance commitment. Such a job will increase intrinsic motivation and, at the same time, will satisfy needs for
growth and achievement.

A former director of recruitment for the United States
Coast Guard said that the branch of the service best known
for loyalty is the Marine Corps. In his opinion, the reason is
that boot camp training constantly challenges Marine re-
cruits to perform beyond their perceived physical limits.
As a result, there is a tremendous pride in passing tests of
rigorous standards and being found capable.

Many managers agree: "The more you challenge people, the more they'll 'pull up' for it. And when they do—
when they actually accomplish the 'impossible'—they will
always be grateful for the experience."

Restructuring jobs so that they offer more autonomy
and challenge is a step many managers can easily take to
increase job satisfaction. And when work is more challenging and interesting, people will work more attentively and
constructively. In my study, I met secretaries on an exciting task force who found themselves eagerly taking home
piles of paper for the first time in their careers. I spoke
with front-line employees who devoted Saturdays to a spe-

cial project because they were "fascinated with the work."

People increase their loyalty when they feel in partnership with their managers—when an alliance is formed
between the workers and their bosses. To facilitate this
kind of bonding, managers must remain aware that their
role has changed from one of "order-giver" to one of coach,
champion, and consensus-builder. Managers who excel at
coaching and delegating give employees control over their
activities and agendas. As one such manager said to me:
"I've finally learned to get out of people's way and off their
backs."

Managers can also develop loyalty by helping people
grow in the direction of their strengths and preferences.
Employees frequently need information regarding opportunities and alternatives within and outside their current
organizations. If they can get this counseling at work—
cross-training, lateral moves, building specific new skills,
career shifts, and so on—their loyalty to the company
increases. If they must seek it elsewhere (and worse, if they
are made to feel disloyal for doing so), a wedge is placed
between them and the company.

Many managers see no need for this division. "My
people need challenges and opportunities. They need to
feel they have control over their career choices and decisions. They also need to be able to move on when it's time.
I cater to those needs."

PAY ATTENTION TO THE EQUITY FACTOR

A close look at the psychology of relationships reveals
that most individuals attempt to keep a mental balance
between what they contribute to a relationship and what
they get out of it. When employees believe that they are
putting more into their company than they are getting
back, or when they do not perceive equitable treatment on
the job, loyalty slips dramatically.

Recently I talked with a stewardess who was having second thoughts about her commitment to the airline. "I've been with this airline for over ten years," she told me. "I've always loved my job and felt like part of the company—as though we were all in this together. I've enjoyed the good times and always understood when salaries or benefits had to be reduced during the hard times. I used to be 'gungo-ho' for this airline. Well, last week I read that our CEO is one of the highest-paid executives in the world; I also know that we just had a very profitable year. But in spite of that, we're being asked to take cuts in health-care and other benefits. For the first time I'm wondering if my loyalty has been misplaced."

At a utilities company, employees were negotiating a 3 percent raise. At the same time, the organization painted their fleet of service trucks and changed the logo. "How dare they quibble about a lousy raise when they're spending tons of money on this junk!" was the sentiment expressed by many employees.

The common issue suggested by these two examples is not just compensation but equity. Like many other issues explored in this book, the idea of equity gains definition in the "eye of the beholder." Fair treatment, in the eyes of the work force, is more often based on individual perceptions of reality rather than on factual information.

Your workers will be more willing to share the downside of "down" times only if they perceive that the burden is shared throughout the company. When Nucor, a steel company in Charlotte, North Carolina, with $1.1 billion in sales, went through tough times, President Ken Iverson took a 60 percent cut in pay.

In many ways, American workers have grown up. They no longer believe in the idea of a paternalistic employer. Seeking greater autonomy, employees have also worked to professionalize their occupations. Many belong to professional associations and societies and are familiar with industry standards for treatment and pay. The employees of today are more educated and informed about their occupations, their organizations, and their rights.

Workers want to be compensated commensurate with others in similar jobs. Management can alleviate employee concern by publishing pay rates and bonuses and comparing them to the industry average. Flexible benefits or "cafeteria" benefits appeal to a diversified work force by allowing employees to choose from equal but different options that meet individual needs.

Beyond equitable compensation, there are several additional ways managers can address the equity issue:

1. Remain objective and impartial in performance appraisals. At the outset, make sure your expectations are clearly understood by employees, then give honest feedback on performance ("This is how I see it") and ask if they agree ("Do you see it differently?").

2. Give credit where it's due. Make sure your acknowlegments are appropriate, timely, and accurate.

3. Display ethical behavior and personal high standards. Demonstrate through your actions that you hold yourself accountable to the same set of standards and performance criteria that you require from others.

4. Increase your sensitivity to areas that might be perceived as inequitable. As a routine part of your decision-making process, ask the question, "Will this be perceived as equitable by others?"

In response to concerns about equity, organizations are doing away with many inequitable practices. Executive parking, private dining rooms, and limited stock options are being replaced by company-wide gatherings, communal eating facilities, and employee stock ownership.

MANAGING FOR LOYALTY THROUGH TRANSITIONS _____

The company is being restructured, maybe taken over by another firm. All top management has been replaced. There are expectations of further cuts and restructurings. And from this damaged body, the work is still expected to flow as if nothing has happened.

Since 1983, according to the Department of Commerce, 4.7 million workers who held jobs for at least three years have been dismissed. Companies are just beginning to appreciate the kind of damage that these massive layoffs can do to morale and productivity.

Every time the drama unfolds, it unfolds before an audience:

"First of all, you see the wrong people getting cut. You know some of these people; they have worked hard and done a good job for the company."

"The way they treated people was awful—with no concern for their feelings. At first I was relieved to be keeping my job, but then I started thinking that it could just as well have been me."

Managers who keep the loyalty of employees know that actions speak louder than words. The people being laid off should be treated with kindness, respect, even solicitude. While that may sound idealistic, in practice it is less a matter of human decency than of hard-nosed pragmatism. The employees who remain will be watching closely to see how those being terminated are treated. When employees are resentful over the loss of their colleagues, or bitter after viewing the way that the outplaced personnel were treated, work often grinds to a standstill for weeks. Anxiety runs high, mistakes are made, and deadlines are missed.

The loyalty of workers who remain is tremendously affected by how they see this sensitive time handled. If they see management taking a callous attitude toward those who are leaving, the remaining employees conclude that they are working for cold, uncaring executives. People keep their heads down and become risk-averse. Loyalty takes a nose dive.

Managers need to understand and facilitate the emotional process that employees go through during this kind of change. It begins with *shock* and *denial*—a time when people generally refuse to acknowledge the situation.

"This can't be happening to me (us)."

"When I came here I was promised . . ."

The stage of denial can be prolonged if employees are not allowed or encouraged to register a reaction, or if management acts as if their reactions to the news are inappropriate. Sometimes managers believe that people are paid to put their feelings aside, that they shouldn't have emotional reactions at work. But this type of thinking, which doesn't address basic emotional considerations, will not change the sequence of responses; it just drives the reactions underground.

Next comes the stage of *anger, negativity, resistance.*

"I didn't have to take this job. I could have gone to . . ."

At this point things seem to get worse. People are filled with self-doubt or anger at the organization. They are forced to contemplate the loss of a job—the loss of income, benefits, privileges, and relationships they have come to rely on. They now face the anxiety of job-hunting, the upheaval of moving to a new location, or the possibility of taking a cut in pay—not to mention the injuries to self-esteem which are inevitable in such situations.

Employees facing major change go through this stage before they become realistic about what the change will mean to their careers.

Management can help facilitate employees' progress by providing a safe forum to express emotions. Let people know that their reactions are natural and expected, and that you understand the difficulties they are going through. Tell them what you will do to continue to support them.

It is also important to remain as factual and informative as possible. Let employees know exactly what they can expect, and help them focus on actual opportunities. It is just as essential to give attention to those employees who are to remain as it is to support those leaving. Everyone in the changing organization goes through a version of this emotional process.

Employees *detach* from the past only after they have been allowed to mourn it. People have been emotionally attached to the old organization and to relationships within it. Recognize and appreciate this attachment as you eulogize the past in the company newsletter, post a pictorial history of the organization on the company bulletin board, or create a formal ceremony to honor "the old days." Only when people have released the past are they ready to investigate the future.

Despite what a company may promise, most employees in organizations that are changing ownership or direction will want to begin looking for new opportunities.

It is important for each individual to assess his skills and background in light of the current job market. Those who have been with a company for a long time are probably unaware of what is available for them in the wider employment world. A thorough assessment of the old job and of future possibilities can prepare employees for making good choices within the new structure.

Some managers build employee loyalty by encouraging subordinates to continually interview for other jobs. A banking vice president, known for his high employee retention, explained this seeming contradiction: "In today's world, we all live with the threat of layoffs. My people can't be productive in this kind of environment unless they know the alternatives and feel secure in their ability to 'survive' the ongoing threat."

The turmoil of restructuring and the ensuing assessment can have a positive outcome. People leaving an organization may explore career potential never before considered; remaining employees may develop a new excitement; the company might be energized by more directed leadership.

During a takeover by one foreign corporation, employees chose to put their sense of loyalty in abeyance until they knew the outcome. "People here are taking a 'wait and see' attitude," the human resources manager told me. "We are trying to help them by communicating the new vision, what and where the new priorities will be, and looking at what these changes mean to their daily behaviors. We are encouraging them to re-enroll and commit their loyalty to the new company."

Commitment is the final phase. At this point employees choose to reinvest their emotional attachment and energies, whether to the same company or to new projects. In one employee's words, "Now it's the time to fall in love with your future." This is a phase during which employees identify with a renewed sense of vision and purpose.

PERSONAL LOYALTY VS. ORGANIZATIONAL LOYALTY

The easiest kind of loyalty to develop is loyalty through personal contact. Most of us have had, at one time or another in our careers, a boss for whom we would gladly go "the extra mile," one for whom we would commit extra time and energy.

Personal loyalty is more immediate and more spontaneous. If bosses hire their own employees, they have already chosen people they like and believe in. They see each other often, share efforts, and may develop strong personal bonds. There is an element of mentorship in training an employee to which both the manager and employee may react with positive personal feelings.

While there are obvious advantages, there are also inherent problems in building personal loyalty into your management-employee relations. In today's business climate of uncertainty, people move in and out of organizations more often than in the past. Since unpredictability in organizational structures is the only certainty, it can be unwise to encourage personal loyalty that requires consistency in relationships.

I spoke with managers who have wrestled with the delicate topic of personal loyalty. They gave insight into the potential problems:

"Encouraging personal loyalty is a disservice to people. It disables them, and when things change and they're upset, they choose not to feel loyal again."

"If employees tell me they want this job because I'm the boss, I am always very clear with them that this is a job where I may not stay, that it is far better for them to choose opportunities independent of personalities."

Encouraging strong personal loyalty can backfire for the manager. An executive for a *Fortune* 500 company was offered the presidency of another company. In his mind, it was "the chance of a lifetime." But when he excitedly told his wife about the proposition, she responded: "Well, of course you won't be able to accept. You have spent the past two years in this position getting people to trust you. You couldn't live with yourself if you left now." After thinking it over, he agreed with her and turned down the job.

In order to focus more closely on organizational loyalty, the manager needs to remind employees that the company is the provider of opportunities and challenges, and that each individual is unified under the corporate mission and goals. Think and talk in terms of company objectives. Position people and efforts in terms of "our" company, with common purpose and even common enemies. Make the relationship between the organization and employees the focus of loyalty, and you will help create a bonding with true team spirit.

The term *team spirit* has become such a cliché that it's difficult to invoke the sense of belonging, thrill of competition, and the joy of victory which it represents. But it is just that kind of excitement and passion which energizes individuals and can transform the workplace.

4 | A CULTURE FOR LOYALTY

COMPETITION

Count Basie was both a great orchestra leader and a great pianist. One night a friend of his, drummer Buddy Rich, took him to Carnegie Hall to hear an incredible new piano player named Peter Nero. Nero's performance was predictably outstanding. Halfway through the concert Count Basie tugged at his collar, leaned over to Buddy Rich and said, "Don't you think it's hot in here?" Rich replied, "Not for drummers."

Accelerated competition for the same customer base has driven organizations through tremendous restructurings. Increasing competition for a shrinking pool of talented workers is making it "hot in here" for many organizations. From the aging of the "baby boom" generation into executive positions to the "seller's job market" created by the "baby bust" work force, demographics brings its own requirements for corporate adjustment. For perhaps the first time in the history of industrialized America, employment opportunities are growing faster than the labor pool.

Demographic statistics show that over the next decade, 80 percent of the entrants in the work force will be women, minorities, and immigrants. This makes the issue of managing diversity—understanding variations in the background and values of this diverse work force—a key item for an organization's agenda.

In 1985, Motorola discovered that 60 percent of their Arlington Heights work force couldn't pass an arithmetic test of questions as simple as "Ten is what percent of 100?" After analysis, it was found that the poor math scores were actually the result of an inability to read or, in the case of many immigrants, to comprehend English.

The mystery was how these people, who were superior employees and had improved quality over tenfold, could do their jobs if they couldn't read. The solution was easy. In the early 1980s, Motorola had several layers of middle managers who acted as translators. By the mid-1980s, however, the company began to remove some of those management layers.

As a result of their findings, Motorola initiated a remedial education program of math and language instruction. Today, the company has a $60 million education budget and a separate account set up to invest in schools that are willing to address the needs of the populations that supply their work force. In addition, in 1989 they opened Motorola University, to make education more relevant to the corporation, to the job, and to the individual. This attention to basic, as well as advanced, training needs will be a concern of many organizations as they tailor education to a diverse group of employees.

The Bureau of Labor Statistics predicts that by the year 2000, females will make up almost 65 percent of the work force. Most of these working women will have children. More than 50 percent will be responsible for the care of aging parents.

Managers who are concerned with retaining talented

female workers are learning to react with flexibility to the concerns of women. Elder- and child-care programs are needed more than ever before. Alternate work patterns such as job-sharing, flextime, and flexplace constitute valuable options for those employees with important considerations beyond the workplace.

The decline in the birth rate in the 1960s and early 1970s means that a smaller number of young people (the baby-bust generation) are entering the job market today. This has created a labor shortage that will worsen in the 1990s. An average of only 1.3 million people will enter the work force every year in the 1990s, down from 3 million during the 1970s. Employers who have known only labor surpluses will soon be bidding for the services of skilled workers.

The first of the baby-bust generation was born in 1965, and they are arriving in corporate America demanding to be treated according to their own rules. These employees insist on getting satisfaction from their jobs, but refuse to make personal sacrifices for the sake of the organization. Other interests—leisure, family, the pursuit of experience—are at least as important as work. They view the stresses on the generations ahead of them and are opting away from workaholism toward "balance" and "wellness." They care about ethical, environmental, and quality-of-life issues.

In *The Affluent Society*, John Kenneth Galbraith defined a New Class—educated, salaried professionals who are seen as valuable to their organizations. These people are twenty-six to forty-five years old, and many were heavily influenced by the social activism and "new age" thinking of the sixties. Nurturing skills and relationship values are the requirements, and the contributions, of women, who constitute a full half of the New Class. Many New Class professionals are also the inner-directed workers of SRI's study. These employees want to contribute to something significant. They want their jobs to have value and meaning.

An intense scramble to get and keep a smaller supply of top talent has already begun. At the same time, organizations are dealing with a highly segmented work force. The use of opinion surveys, questionnaires, focus groups, and one-on-one interviews will be increasingly important for "taking the pulse" of diverse audiences in order to understand their unique needs, desires, and value systems. Corporations with a competitive edge are those whose cultures are flexible and responsible to variety.

THE NEW CONTRACT

> "Loyalty needs to be conscious, based on shared values and benefits between the employee and the organization."
> —Sue Swenson, Area Vice President,
> Pacific Bell

The loyalty contract has always existed in American business as a real, if unwritten, set of expectations regarding the manifestations of mutual loyalty. Since both employees and their organizations have changed, a new loyalty contract which clearly states the roles and responsibilities of each party can facilitate the development of a shared vision.

The new contract begins with a primary question asked at the corporate level: "Is loyalty an important factor in the organization's success?"

If the answer is "yes," then the next step is to ask: "What measurable behaviors constitute employee loyalty? How have we communicated these to the work force?" and "Are the existing corporate policies and procedures showing loyalty to employees in ways they understand and value? How do we know this?"

To develop organizational loyalty, the ingredients of a

loyal relationship must be built into operating procedures and made a key part of the culture. American corporations often adopt a short-term, quarter-to-quarter outlook and business strategy in which each quarter must look better than the last. Organizations with a reputation for employee loyalty adopt a longer-range view in which loyalty results from established attitudes and practices that offer stability within a continuity of purpose.

For the last four years, pharmaceutical giant Merck has scored highest among 305 of the largest U.S. companies evaluated by thousands of top executives, directors, and security analysts participating in *Fortune* magazine's annual survey. Merck placed first in innovativeness, quality of products, quality of management, use of corporate assets, and value as a long-term investment. It also ranked number one in its ability to attract, develop, and keep talented people.

At Merck, loyalty is addressed consciously. From benefit packages to a wide array of training and development programs, Merck goes out of its way to satisfy employees. Even though the company has gone through no major restructuring, Merck is not the same paternalistic organization of fifteen or twenty years ago. Now it provides employees with the resources to work independently.

Merck also has definite requirements of the work force, and these expectations are clearly outlined: Employees are expected to contribute to the growth of the company; to respect company goals; to treat others fairly; to adhere to safety, quality, and ethical standards which are detailed by specific policies and behaviors in the employee handbook; and to keep skills up-to-date. Public and community involvement is also highly publicized and recommended.

In an entirely different industry and geographic location, Colorado National Bank also gives conscious attention to the subject of loyalty. The president of the company,

Dale Browning, says that loyalty is shown to employees by clearly communicating the mission and philosophy of the organization, by treating employees fairly, challenging them to grow into their potential, recognizing them as individuals, and rewarding their successes.

In return, employees are expected to display loyalty by contributing to the goals of the company. To facilitate this, they are asked to communicate with and assist others, even across departmental lines. Further, they are encouraged to contribute to the community.

Organizations insure loyalty when they make an "upfront" commitment to their people. The new loyalty contract needs clearly outlined and communicated goals, benefits, and expectations to which employees can respond.

VISIONARY LEADERSHIP

"The CEO's main responsibility is to communicate the mission."

—George Hoyt, President and CEO,
Lesher Communications

Top management can present a clear, compelling picture of the organization's mission and of the strategies by which its objectives are to be achieved. "Keep the vision simple, but elevated," observes Reuben Mark, CEO of Colgate. "You're never going to get anyone to charge the machine guns only for financial gain. It's got to be something that makes people feel better, feel a part of something bigger than themselves."

Apple's vision to change the world through technology motivates and inspires people who have a similar outlook on the positive applications of computer science. Rallying employees behind this vision bonds them to a common cause. Management at Apple develops loyalty by showing employees how their contributions are important in realizing company goals.

Motorola's fundamental objective is to insure "total customer satisfaction." Employees carry a plastic card with an imprinted reminder that corporate goals will not be achieved without the total commitment and effort of each employee. Colgate's rallying cry is simply "We can be the best." Individuals are encouraged to do their best for a company which has the ultimate goal of providing an outstanding product.

S. C. Johnson Wax has amended their corporate mission statement (a full document entitled "This We Believe") to include an environmental mission statement. It reads, in part: "The greatest challenge that we face together today is making those vital decisions that will determine the quality of life for ensuing generations. We will display leadership in pursuit of this challenge by bringing to all of our customers major technological innovations in our product packaging, formulation and manufacturing that promote clean air, clean water and clean earth—a healthier, safer environment for us all."

Once the vision has been developed, top management than continually reinforces it by elaborating, interpreting, and giving it immediate relevance. Founder Konosuke Matsushita's 250-year vision for his company was summed up in the "Seven Spirits of Matsushita," to which he referred constantly in his policy statements. Each January he kept the core vision alive by weaving one-year operational objectives into an annual theme that was then captured in a slogan. In this way he kept the lofty corporate purpose from becoming abstract. His employees had concrete guidance in implementing Matsushita's goals.

VALUES

> "As time goes by, talking about values will be regarded as absolutely essential—just as essential as marketing or logistics or strategic planning or thinking or decision-making."
>
> —Richard Zimmerman, Chairman and CEO,
> Hershey Food Corporation

To capture employee loyalty requires a consistent, coherent, and carefully developed set of values. The first priority is to recruit people who embrace the same value system. To insure this, values are clearly explained and the interview process is structured to determine the candidate's willingness to become part of the company's culture. Only then are credentials considered.

At a Northern California insurance company, every employee (even the part-time clerical staff) is paid a regular salary plus an incentive based on performance. As a result, the firm attracts go-getters who push themselves into high earnings. In the hiring interview, the manager tells a potential employee that the office is filled with high-energy people, many of whom ask for overtime projects. He makes it clear that workers who prefer a "regular" nine-to-five job may find themselves uncomfortable in these hectic surroundings. People can "select out" if they don't want to work in that kind of environment.

In their orientation booklet, Apple tells a story of three people laying bricks. They are each asked to describe their job. The first person says that he is laying bricks. The second person states that he is building a wall. The third worker reports that he is creating a cathedral. Apple lets potential employees know that they want people who create cathedrals.

Motorola shows potential employees a video in which the company's values are explained. This includes everything from the key values—uncompromising integrity and a constant respect for others—to daily expectations, such as a drug-free culture. Understanding these values and expectations helps people self-screen before they sign up.

Through Hewlett-Packard's Student Employment and Education Development Program, the company identifies potential employees while they are still in college. H-P gives these students summer internships and exposes them to organizational values during the school year by sending them company newsletters.

Apple spends two full days showing new people exactly what it will be like to work there. They go through a simulation of an Apple project, stressing those values and approaches which are desirable.

The Equitable Finance Companies publish a "Policy Statement on Ethics" to reaffirm the ethical values with which the company identifies. It reminds all agents and employees of their personal responsibility for maintaining honest, fair, and legal business practices in working with clients, suppliers, the public, and each other.

Respect for the individual, ethical conduct, integrity, and commitment to excellence—these are values with which we can all identify. When an organization's values reflect those of the work force, employees are proud to be associated with the company, and their loyalty increases.

Alexander B. Horniman is the director of the Center for the Study of Applied Ethics at the University of Virginia's Darden School of Business. He suggests a simple process for testing an organization's value system: Ask employees what principles they would be fired for violating. If they can't think of anything beyond "Thou shalt not steal," don't expect much in the way of values. If, on the other hand, they can cite a few that command your respect, then you just may have found a company worth being loyal to.

CONGRUENT COMMUNICATION SYSTEMS _____

> "The essential organizational tool for building loyalty is communication."
> —R. E. Rhody, Director of Corporate Communications,
> Bank of America

An organization communicates formally through its annual reports, newsletters, magazines, videotapes, and meetings. It communicates informally through behaviors, actions, interactions, and even inactions. When employees perceive a gap between formal words and actions, feelings of loyalty and trust weaken.

Formal communication is what the organization says is important. Informal communication is what people in the organization do to indicate issues of importance. Communicating for loyalty requires building congruence between formal and informal systems.

The founder of Wal-Mart, Sam Walton, along with his top managers, built loyalty and motivation in 215,000 employees, many of them unskilled workers with starting pay of less than $5 an hour. The company began with an organization-wide campaign entitled "We Care." In order to communicate this message in actions, Wal-Mart did the following:

1. Everyone at Wal-Mart became an "associate."

2. "We," "us," "our" became the operative words.

3. Hourly associates along with their department heads were privy to figures regarding costs, freight charges, and profit margins.

4. The company set a profit goal for each store, and if the store exceeded it, the hourly associates shared part of the additional profit.

5. The organization's profit-sharing plan (to which Wal-Mart contributed 6.4 percent of an eligible employee's

wages in 1988) was invested principally in Wal-Mart stock.

6. Partnership was also expressed in open-door policies and grass-roots meetings, designed to give each individual the opportunity to talk over concerns and problems.

Few actions speak louder to employees than the personal involvement of senior management. When British Airways conducted its "Putting People First" program, Sir Colin Marshall, CEO, attended 74 percent of the sessions—scattered around the world—to lend his personal support to the ideas taught in the training.

Jim, John, and Bruce Nordstrom answer their own mail and telephones. They spend their most productive time on the floor of a Nordstrom store talking to front-line employees. "We invite employee input. Nothing is more important than having employees know they have access to us at any time."

When Fred Gibbons, CEO at Software Publishing, wanted to communicate equitable employee treatment, he took off the door to his office. He also eliminated special parking privileges and saw to it that all company desks were the same size. He held himself accountable to the same set of rules as all other employees because he believed that the boss should be a "walking example."

When corporations want to shape communications, technology can be invaluable. When Donald Petersen was CEO of Ford, the company maintained an in-house television network to broadcast a steady stream of up-to-the-minute company news and announcements from the chairman. Bethlehem Steel, during its drastic downsizing, beamed a constantly updated electronic newsletter to every employee within peering distance of a computer.

Still, the communication medium of choice is a personal appearance by a senior manager, preferably one who will field questions from the audience. Many companies choose these emissaries carefully. At some organizations, the personnel department holds auditions for the part.

SELF-FULFILLMENT AT WORK

> "What is extraordinary about the search for self-fulfillment in contemporary America is that it is not confined to a few bold spirits or a privileged class. Cross-section studies of Americans show unmistakably that the search for self-fulfillment is instead an outpouring of popular sentiment and experimentation, an authentic grass-roots phenomenon involving, in one way or the other, perhaps as many as 80 percent of all adult Americans. It is as if tens of millions of people had decided simultaneously to conduct risky experiments in living, using the only materials that lay at hand—their own lives."
>
> —Daniel Yankelovich, *New Rules*

At work, the search for self-fulfillment takes on profound importance as people seek jobs that are challenging, empowering, and rewarding to them in all aspects of their lives. Companies in tune with this dynamic are initiating innovative measures to insure that their people stay productive and personally fulfilled.

Herman Miller, Inc., a company which is consistently mentioned on lists of the best places to work, offers an employee Bill of Rights:

- The right to be needed: genuine opportunities to utilize talents.

- The right to be understood: ongoing communication about what is happening in the company.

- The right to be involved: invitations to each employee to contribute ideas, and the guarantee of a response.

- The right to a contractual relationship: agreed-upon objectives and negotiation of conflicts and differences.

- The right to affect one's destiny: involvement of people in decisions that impact their lives.

- The right to be held accountable: the opportunity to contribute and to have those contributions measured according to previously established standards.

- The right to appeal: a check against unfair or arbitrary exercise of power.

The employee Bill of Rights at Herman Miller empowers the work force by defining its rights and obligations and therefore outlining a path to individual fulfillment.

W. L. Gore & Associates, the maker of Gortex and other products, is a high-tech firm that grosses over $300 million a year. Bill Gore, the founder, who died in 1986, organized the company around his philosophy of business: "To get rich and to have fun."

To keep Gore's work atmosphere intimate and personal, no one plant is allowed to have more than two hundred workers. As the organization grows, new plants are opened. Instead of bosses, associates have "sponsors" who act as friends and mentors. There are no formal hierarchies or job titles except those people create for themselves. Small work teams take charge of themselves, deciding how to do the job while remaining responsible for output. People work in an innovative, caring, and "fun" environment, working on projects to which they are personally committed.

While there is a lack of well-defined, clearly presented management philosophy at most organizations, there doesn't have to be. Consider how Johnson & Johnson's well-known corporate policies address the issue of employee self-fulfillment:

- We are responsible to our employees, the men and women who work with us throughout the world.
- Everyone must be considered an individual.
- We must recognize their dignity and recognize their merit. They must have a sense of security in their jobs.

- Compensation must be fair and adequate, and working conditions clean, orderly, and safe.
- Employees must feel free to make suggestions and complaints.
- There must be equal opportunity for employment, development, and advancement for those qualified.
- We must provide competent management, and their actions must be just and ethical.

ServiceMaster Limited Partnership is an international manager of support-service workers. (Among other things, they manage housekeeping services for hospitals.) As identified in the corporate philosophy, their first organizational objective is "to honor God in all we do." One way this is expressed at ServiceMaster is in management's efforts to bring dignity and self-fulfillment to people at work.

All ServiceMaster managers and executives (including the CEO) have regular "service assignments," where they join workers in the field, so that they continually understand and empathize with the realities of the job. At hospitals, monthly "council sessions" feature department heads explaining the important role that cleanliness has in contributing to the wellness of patients—helping hospital workers relate beyond the mechanics of the job to the larger issue of their role in saving lives.

Quality-of-worklife programs and employee self-fulfillment issues are top priorities at an increasing number of companies across the United States. A few examples:

- Ford Motor Company operates one of the most extensive employee involvement programs in the country.
- Xerox has been experimenting since 1980 with ways to give its employees a greater voice in day-to-day decisions.
- Bank of America offers planning, coaching, and evalua-

tion systems designed to help managers steer the careers of their people.

- Pacific Northwest Bell uses a computerized job skills bank to help employees locate the "right" job opportunities within the company.

- Federal Express, Citicorp, and Borg-Warner Company are among the one hundred companies that use peer review boards to help resolve employee grievances.

- Apple urges employees to be loyal to themselves first, then to see how the company fits into their goals.

Employee empowerment finds full expression in the Nordstrom employee handbook. Because it illustrates the type of organizational approach which is successful in encouraging employee fulfillment through participation, I've quoted it in its entirety:

> Welcome to Nordstrom. We're glad to have you with our company. Our number one goal is to provide outstanding service. Set both your personal and professional goals high. We have great confidence in your ability to achieve them. Nordstrom Rules: Rule #1—Use your good judgement in all situations. There will be no additional rules. Please feel free to ask your department manager, store manager, or division general manager any question at any time.

In Fremont, California, NUMI (New United Motors) Auto Plant is jointly owned by General Motors and Toyota. They operate under a unique agreement with the United Auto Workers, which states: "Workers and managers together are doing things differently based upon an understanding and respect, rather than coercion and contempt." The difference is that management and employees work together to create a satisfying work environment in which the requirements of self-fulfillment are part of the agreement.

EMPOWERING EMPLOYEES

"No matter what your business, high-performance teams are the wave of the future."
—Jerry Junkins, CEO, Texas Instruments

Employees today are seeking more freedom of choice, more authority, and (especially at lower levels) more ownership of their work. Many companies have granted employees the power to make major decisions on the job, and have gained more motivated, productive, and committed workers in return. An example is Ford Motor Company and the United Auto Workers, who have inaugurated a worker participation program, called Employee Involvement (EI), to improve productivity and quality, as well as worker environment. Foremen at Ford's Edison plant chat and joke with employees, solicit their ideas, and encourage them to stop assembly lines when defects are spotted. As a result, quality has gone up, absenteeism has been reduced, and personnel are happier.

Eastman Kodak put hourly workers in charge of "13 Room"—an operation that manufactures professional film. Employees were given the power to make purchasing decisions, start or stop the assembly line, and design the equipment to suit their needs. In 1988, 13 Room ran $1 million over its $30 million budget. In 1989, with workers in charge, the unit came in $1.5 million under budget.

Here are some other examples of successful employee participation:

- Herman Miller, the designer and manufacturer of office furniture, treats its 5,400 workers as participants in a shared enterprise. Employees are organized into self-managed teams and earn quarterly bonuses based on benchmarks that take into account the ideas they have contributed.

- At a General Mills plant in Lodi, California, teams schedule, operate, and maintain machinery so effectively that the factory runs with no managers present during the night shift.

- Teams of blue-collar workers convinced CEO Ralph Stayer to enlarge the Johnsonville Foods plant so they could produce more sausage. Since 1986 production has risen at least 50 percent.

- At a weekly meeting, a group of Federal Express clerks spotted—and eventually solved—a billing problem that was costing the company $2.1 million a year.

Employees' need to learn new skills, and to take control of that process, is pivotal to the success of a unique employee involvement project at S. C. Johnson Wax in Racine, Wisconsin. Last year I was invited to speak at the annual dinner meeting of the Office Support Network (OSN). Conceived during a 1985 company participation workshop by a group of office staff workers who decided there was a need for an organization to promote professional and personal growth, the Office Support Network now has a ten-member steering committee and nine subcommittees. Through surveying the four hundred people who work in office support jobs at the company, the Changes in Office Environment Committee tries to identify changing trends in job requirements and skills. The Training and Development Committee offers two to four programs per year. These programs respond to needs identified in annual surveys and are chosen (and sometimes designed) by the committee itself. One committee manages the *Network News* newsletter, another is responsible for a biannual updating of the office reference manual, and still another committee identifies computer applications which are of benefit to OSN members. The Library Committee reviews and purchases books, periodicals, and audiovisual materials. The Annual Dinner Meeting Committee hosts the event at which I spoke. The chairwoman of the OSN steering committee, also a senior library clerk, contacted me and made all the financial and travel arrangements for the engagement. She later told me: "It's given me a whole new view of myself. I now know how to conduct meetings and give speeches. It's improved my professionalism and increased my pride in the company."

HEALTHY COMPANIES

> "A work force that can physically and mentally withstand whatever the business climate brings can weather any boom, recession, depression, merger, takeover, or expansion."
>
> —William Kizer, CEO,
> Central States Health and Life

Today's workers are better educated to know what lifestyle factors and company influences can make them healthier. A healthy, highly motivated work force is critical for a productive, competitive company. Organizations that create healthy work environments are responding to the evolving concerns of their employees. These companies may also increase profitability by lowering the cost of health and disability insurance bills and by decreasing absenteeism. Here are some of the innovative programs and policies that organizations are initiating to insure that their people stay healthy and productive:

- Northern Telecom's Health Enhancement Program offers employees help on everything from quitting smoking to controlling blood pressure and losing weight.

- Franklin Life Insurance provides prenatal health education programs at the work site.

- Levi Strauss & Company offers education and support on

AIDS in a number of different ways, from lectures for managers to resource and support classes for individuals with AIDS, their families and friends.

- Safeway Stores Bakery Division built its own fitness facility, performs exercise assessments on all employees, and runs a "Health in Humor" clinic.

- Fisher Price's production line workers rotate every two hours to avoid boredom.

- IBM has redesigned factory carts to prevent back strain, supplied workers with rubber hand tools to prevent wrist cramps, and redesigned video display terminals to reduce glare and eyestrain.

Balancing Work and Family

> "Integrating family life and work isn't just good for people, it makes good business sense."
> —Nancy Evans, President, Doubleday & Company

While people want to be emotionally involved in work which has meaning, many are also reevaluating the issue of balancing work with family life. They are earnest about being involved with their children and with each other. Organizations which address family issues and support special programs will build loyalty and commitment in the work force.

When Nancy Evans first started out in publishing, older women used to say to her: "Well, you're never going to have a child, are you? That'll wreck your career."

She finally did choose to have a baby while working at the Gannet Company, an organization known for progressive corporate policies dealing with family issues. "With so much technology available, there are new ways of doing things so that the business doesn't have to stop when a woman has a baby. During the last few weeks of my pregnancy we set up a fax machine at my home, brought in an assistant, and held meetings there."

Many companies are setting positive examples in this area:

- Tel-Pro, Inc., established the Triple R Ranch, a summer camp for children, after noticing increased absenteeism among working parents during the summer.

- Baxter Travenol Laboratories prepares educational kits for children who have been uprooted because of a parent's relocation.

- Hewlett-Packard has a flexible policy that allows time off for vacation, personal business, child care, or to tend a sick relative.

- AT&T's new employee contract establishes a $5 million Family Care Development Fund to provide money for the creation of community-based child- and elder-care facilities.

- Merck offers a liberal parental leave (up to eighteen months), day-care-center support, company-wide child-care referral, "Family Matters" workshops, employee assistance, and a career search workshop for employees' family members.

- Genentech Inc. owns one of the largest corporate day-care centers in the country. The company pays half of the cost of full-time day care for employee children of ages six weeks to six years.

- Johnson Wax created a position entitled "manager of Quality of Life," whose function is to design enriching programs in after-work activities for employees and their families. Johnson employees are also invited to use the corporate-owned 146-acre park—complete with softball diamond, miniature golf course, aquatic center, and fully equipped gym.

RECOGNITION PROGRAMS _____

"Want to amaze your employees? Tell them you like their work."

—Daniel C. Boyle, Daniel C.
Boyle & Associates

In 1980, after a grievance meeting with union representatives, Dan Boyle (then personnel manager of the Palmer Plant for Diamond International Corporation) noticed that only a few of the items discussed were true grievances. The other issues were minor matters that had escalated into larger problems because of poor working relationships. To improve morale, communication, and productivity, he suggested instituting a program that would recognize and reward those employees who were doing their jobs well. This was the modest beginning of "The 100 Club," an approach that would later be the subject of articles in *Time* magazine and the *Harvard Business Review*.

The 100 Club concept involves a reward system developed and administered through a voluntary labor-management committee. Workers accumulate points for such things as attendance, punctuality, work safety, and suggestions that save money. Employees who earn 100 points receive a jacket and become eligible to redeem merchandise, from quartz watches to binoculars, with additional earned points.

At the Palmer Plant, which manufactures egg cartons, The 100 Club was launched in 1981. After its first year, the company saved $5.2 million, productivity increased 14.5 percent, and quality-related mistakes dropped by 40 percent. By 1986, for an annual cost of approximately $20 per employee, the company had a return of more than 250 times its original investment, measurable through increased productivity, reduced absenteeism, and a decreased number of industrial accidents. Most significantly, the relationship between management and labor improved; there was a new team spirit that had a positive effect on all aspects of production.

Although skeptics may wonder how a $35 nylon jacket can improve productivity, the workers who get awards say the recognition, not the monetary value of the product, is the key motivational factor.

One Diamond employee was proudly displaying her baby-blue jacket with its company logo and "The 100 Club" emblem. "My employer gave it to me for doing a good job," she said. "This is the first time in the eighteen years I've been there that they have recognized me for the things I do every day."

It touches people emotionally to know their efforts are appreciated. They value items that symbolize the appreciation. They want to be recognized in front of their peers. While American business tends to emphasize the logical, some organizations are beginning to understand and harness the power of emotion. The greatest reward a company can offer is one that says to people: "We love what you are doing."

As the labor pool shrinks, more companies are rewarding those employees who best help the firm meet its goals. From "thank you"s posted on the bulletin board to "Hall of Fame" photos, and "Employee of the Month" designations to formal awards, recognition programs are in action across the country.

North Face Company, a California manufacturer of high-quality outdoor equipment, recognizes pattern cutters with "The Golden Shears" award.

Colgate-Palmolive Company honored nineteen employees at its annual dinner by giving them $3,500 in stock, a gold medal, and an embroidered jacket.

Omni Hotels honors their "Service Champions" with a three-day celebration. Champions are line employees who have been seen by management, and/or mentioned frequently by guests, as having performed outstanding customer services. These top people are further rewarded with medals, cash awards, and a drawing for a trip anywhere in the world.

American Express Company's Travel Related Services recognized forty-three employees as "Great Performers" and rewarded them with up to $4,800 in traveler's checks and a platinum pin.

In 1988, according to *Premium Incentives Business* magazine, companies spent $215.9 million on non-sales employee incentive programs. This represents an increase of 5.7 percent from the year before. And these figures are expected to continue rising. In terms of productivity and loyalty, the money spent is a sound investment.

American Airlines saved almost $31.5 million last year through its employee suggestion program. If an employee's idea makes or saves money for the airline, that person earns credits redeemable for merchandise, travel, cars, and cash.

Heekin Can in Cincinnati, maker of metal cans, has used The 100 Club program since 1984, and says absenteeism among its 850-member work force declined from 4 percent to between 1 and 1.5 percent. Ray Sheppard, vice president of public relations at Heekin, is sold on the multitude of positive results: "Quite frankly, I've never seen anything like it in a union setting."

Tying employees to the success of their organization is a sure method of increasing productivity, commitment, and loyalty. At the same time, if business is down and across-the-board cuts are imminent, employees are more likely to understand that they must take partial responsibility for failures.

Bank of America is a recent example of employees being acknowledged for organizational success. B of A was, for a number of years, the largest bank in the world. Then it began to lose heavily in various loans. Meanwhile, its retail division was suffering through rapidly shifting policies. By the mid-eighties Bank of America closed many departments, changed CEOs, and had even sold its headquarters building in San Francisco.

No longer among the top ten banks in the world, B of A began a comeback. When they posted their second profitable year, analysts relented and stock rebounded. At this point, Bank of America gave away ten shares of stock to each of 53,000 employees.

Duncan Knowles, vice president of organizational communications, commented: "Our management wanted to recognize employees, and to show appreciation for past sacrifices and efforts in turning this company around. Management wanted to give employees not just money, but ownership in the company. You should have seen the effect. It was overwhelming. Kids in the mailroom who had never owned any kind of stock suddenly thought of themselves as capitalists. One clerk said: 'Now that I'm one of the owners, I'm going to start watching paper clips.' Our CEO was flooded with positive thank-you letters and calls at corporate headquarters. It was a tremendous morale boost."

Thomas Tyrrell, CEO of American Steel & Wire, believes that employees will apply themselves to making an organization succeed only if they have a stake in its welfare. At American Steel & Wire, all employees, including the CEO, receive the same benefits, whether vacation, profit-sharing, or health insurance. "The feeling is that," says Tyrrell, "if we make it, we all make it together."

Many companies now have an employee stock ownership plan (ESOP) which rewards workers with a share of the profits when they retire. But some organizations go even further. At Allied Plywood in Alexandria, Virginia, employees own 100 percent of the company and receive up to one-third of the gross profits in their paychecks every month. In some years, the profit portion of their pay amounts to $10,000. The results: Customer service is first rate, absenteeism is so low it's "hard to measure," output is as high as at other companies with double the number of Allied's eighty-four employees, and loyalty to the company goals and objectives is readily apparent.

To clearly connect effort with reward, many companies set aside a pool of money for management to use in awarding spot bonuses to employees who achieve exceptional results. Wells Fargo Bank gave this concept an innovative twist when sixteen thousand employees were each given awards of $35 to present to a co-worker. This peer-to-peer recognition had two distinct advantages: (1) The employees knew better than their bosses who actually deserved a special acknowledgment, and (2) for each $35 spent, two people felt great!

Another incentive program gaining wide acceptance is "pay-for-performance." Leonard A. Schlesinger, associate professor at Harvard Business School, observes: "The pay-for-performance trend is occurring at all corporate levels. There are few better ways to get people moving in the right direction."

It appears he may be right. At First Service Bank, an employee job-training program linked promotions, raises, and bonuses to job performance. Within a year, assets were up 70 percent, productivity increased 25 percent, and turnover was down by half.

Pay-for-performance may be any one (or a combination) of the following plans:

Individual incentive. Payment is directly related to the meeting of individual goals, as in piecework.

Lump-sum payment. A one-time reward, based on individual performance.

Exception stock options. Grants of stock or stock options to nonmanagement employees not usually eligible.

Profit-sharing. A uniform payment based on corporate earnings, given to all employees.

Gain-sharing. Plans that reward productivity of a unit or division.

Small-group incentive. A one-time reward to all members of a group, based on their reaching a predetermined objective.

Pay-for-knowledge. A pay plan that is based on skills or jobs mastered.

At the Lincoln Electric Company, the pay-for-performance philosophy is taken to heart like nowhere else. Located in Cleveland, the company produces arc-welding machinery and electric motors. Each worker is paid based on what he produces. He must repair work defects on his own time. To encourage innovation, the company locks itself into piecework rates. If a worker improves his production methods, the company does not refigure the rate— regardless of how dramatically volume rises and enriches the worker.

The average line worker at Lincoln makes $45,000. Last year, one zealot pulled in $97,000. Employee turnover is a mere 3 percent, including retirements.

Management *can* create a corporate culture that demonstrates sensitivity and loyalty—from extensive compensation packages to sabbaticals for long-term employees, from policies encouraging promotion within the company to praise for a job well done—practices which employees understand and appreciate.

LOYALTY IN JAPAN

"Most of the people we talk to are interested in more challenging work and responsibility, a freer, happier work environment, and the right location."
—Akira Nakaya, headhunter in Tokyo

An article in the Japanese-language edition of *Newsweek* declared that the image of the Japanese as an intensely hard-working group who submerge their individuality and sacrifice their emotions for the sake of efficiency is fast crumbling.

The Japanese magazine *Da Capo* asked in a cover story: "What is a Super Salaryman?" Instead of describing a traditional worker who slavishly spouts maxims about company solidarity, the lengthy article declared that the characteristics of an up-to-date worker have "nothing at all to do with loyalty to some foolish company." *Da Capo* goes on to describe the enviable situation of the American "salaryman" who "enters a company whenever he likes after graduating from college, thinks nothing of changing jobs, and doesn't consider himself a cog in a company machine, but rather a single, independent laborer under contract."

What is happening to Japanese loyalty?

Obviously, not all Japanese are rushing to embrace the individualism expressed by the magazine articles. In fact, the vast majority are simply uninterested in abandoning the security of their companies to face the uncertainties of life on their own. To the traditional salaryman (white-collar worker), the employer provides his personal identity. The answer to "What do you do?" does not require a description of a job function, merely the name of a company ("I work for ———"). Company prestige becomes individual prestige. Loyalty is taken for granted.

But although these new developments are gradual and marginal, they carry profound implications for the future of the Japanese organization.

The full Japanese employment system, with guaranteed tenure, company housing, and payment based on seniority, has only ever been granted to a minority (under 30 percent) of the work force. It was never offered in small or entrepreneurial companies, and never to female workers. Still, the practice influenced the psychology of work in Japan as typified by loyalty, self-sacrifice, and group harmony.

Just as in the West, changes in corporate loyalty are being driven by forces on both sides of the contract.

During the years of industrial expansion in the 1960s, many new salaried workers were hired. Now there is a glut of employees in their mid-forties, who are vying for the very few top management positions. Hoping to break the bottleneck that is plaguing middle-management levels and keeping bright, younger employees from assuming management responsibilities, Japanese companies are offering inducements to middle-aged workers to take early retirements.

For the first time, employees are looking to job switches as a way of dealing with their frustration about the slowness of promotion at their companies. At the same time, hundreds of companies in Tokyo are seeking experienced executives and professionals (such as engineers and biotechnology researchers) to help them diversify into new markets. Headhunting and job-hopping have become accepted parts of a changing job market.

A recent study by Recruit Company revealed that 25 percent of more than ten thousand white-collar employees surveyed have changed jobs in the past three years. Another 38.5 percent are considering a move.

Increasingly, leaders of Japanese organizations are expressing feelings of being burdened by the seniority system. A more exacting world is forcing them to recognize real ability, rather than just seniority. Adopting a practice that was all but unknown in the past, Japanese companies, such as Sumitomo Trust and Banking Company, are now implementing "lone wolf expert" programs. That is, they are hiring individual talented workers on a contractual basis.

Out of fear of losing their best potential managers, Japanese companies are starting to put a higher premium on merit as well. Employee response to this varies with the generations: Older salarymen are aghast to find cutthroat competition invading the group harmony, but many of the younger generation are jubilant.

This younger generation (dubbed the "new humans" by their elders) are bringing a different set of values to the workplace. A succession of surveys by government agencies and the mass media chart changes in the attitudes of young salarymen. The results show that younger Japanese differ from their elders in that young workers are:

- More motivated by money.

- Convinced they have little chance of reaching the top of the organizational pyramid.

- Impatient deferring to possibly less creative older men.

- Interested in building friendships and interests outside of work.

- Less interested in following orders and more interested in mastering a specialist knowledge.

- Willing to contemplate changing companies to improve their lot.

The founder of one executive search firm in Japan noted: "What employees want from the company has changed. If they don't get things like vacations, good promotions, and good pay, they will switch their loyalty when given the opportunity."

With the upheavals brought on by the trade surpluses and the rising yen, modern Japanese salarymen have learned that not everyone in the world works so hard, commutes such long hours, or remains at the same company from college graduation until retirement. Many say they are eager—in a way that would have been unthinkable twenty years ago—to be relieved of these Japanese corporate traditions.

5 | THE NEW LOYALTY

A PARADIGM SHIFT

"In times of rapid change, our past experience is our worst enemy."

—J. Paul Getty

A paradigm is a set of beliefs which governs the rules and boundaries for success. In some ways a paradigm is like a box. Here is an example: Do you recall the first time you saw the nine-dot puzzle? Do you remember why it was so difficult to solve?

The goal of the puzzle is to connect the dots with four intersecting straight lines without lifting the pen from the paper. Most people find it difficult to solve because they struggle to stay within the "box" formed by the dots. The solution is easy to see when one realizes he can go outside the box.

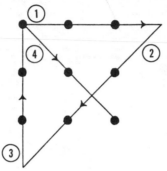

The organizational paradigm of the business world has shifted from one which stresses permanent commitments to one which understands that most professional relationships are temporary. For a time in modern industrial society, organizations were considered "families." According to the old paradigm, membership in the organizational "family" was dependent on staying in the company's good graces and behaving according to established norms and rigid rules. To succeed under the new paradigm, people must move their thinking "outside of the box" and question antiquated beliefs about employment, organizational structures, and loyalty.

Today it is more effective to think in terms of flexible "temporary systems"—much like a sports team or a movie company. Peter Drucker states: "The basic realization is that everybody today is a volunteer." While people need a job and a paycheck, they also have greater mobility. Like an actor or a director, employees can "walk off the set" at any time.

Gene Hackman is an Academy Award-winning actor. Interviewed on the set of a movie he was making, Mr. Hackman had this to say about temporary systems: "There is an opportunity for intensity in work, for closeness in working relationships, and for mutual commitment to a common goal. It is exciting and full."

Temporary systems by their very nature are relatively short-term liaisons between people with a common purpose. These fast-paced, new systems require a strong commitment, trust, and mutual expressions of loyalty for them to be successful. In the old "family" paradigm, workers might hold onto the security of employment in exchange for a lifetime of blind loyalty. This system doesn't do justice to the growth potential of organizations or of individuals in a rapidly changing business climate. As a result, people are beginning to recognize the benefits of adopting the temporary-system outlook. At Johnson Wax, a privately held company in the Midwest, one worker said candidly: "I wish we'd stop referring to this as a family. It's not. It's a business. But that doesn't mean we can't care about each other and show mutual respect."

THE NEW SECURITY

"If security no longer comes from being employed, then it must come from being employable."
—Rosabeth Moss Kanter, *When Giants Learn to Dance*

Present training and experience can make a person more employable in the future marketplace. Since job security itself is uncertain, the acquisition of new skills can be an important ingredient to another kind of security—in the form of "employability."

An organization can attract bright, energetic people by marketing itself as a place to become more employable. How could you use the employability issue to best position your company in the minds of today's talented workers? Consider these "sales" points:

1. What are the specific advantages to an employee of being part of your organization? Does the company offer the chance to work on the leading edge of an industry, the opportunity to take on more management responsibility, or to broaden technical skills?

2. In what ways does the organization enhance its employees' employability by investing in the training and development of its workers? Does your organization offer special education or training that can be added to an employment résumé?

3. How does your organization build the professional reputation of its talented workers? Does the company help people make a name for themselves by publicly recognizing their achievements and plugging them into professional networks?

THE NEW LEADERSHIP

"A leader is one who serves."

—Lao-tzu

Requirements for today's leaders go even beyond the wise and compassionate use of power in the service of others. Today's employees are looking for leadership that is also motivating and inspiring. Everything leaders do and say teaches others how to behave. Their words and actions can enhance loyalty or inhibit it—perhaps even prevent loyalty from developing. "New leaders" build loyalty when they do the following:

Become a champion of change. Change is no longer an element of the environment. It *is* the environment. New leaders respond to change proactively—looking for opportunities and making people aware of future challenges.

Leaders create change, adapt to change, and control change by finding ways to make it serve them and their organizations.

They are also aware that others may have difficulties accepting change. Leaders minimize this resistance by communicating change early on, supporting the change with finances and necessary skills training, breaking overwhelming change into manageable pieces, and giving people control over the change process. They sell and persuade, rather than issue orders for change.

Take risks. New leaders take risks and encourage others to do so, knowing that risk-taking is vital to ultimate success. They are decisive. They are, however, not infallible. They accept full responsibility for risks that fail. When they make an error, they admit that they were wrong. By publicly accepting the consequences of making mistakes, they show others how to learn from experience. Risk-taking—even when it fails—then becomes an opportunity for personal growth.

Promote a personal vision. New leaders operate from a clearly defined set of personal and company goals. They are loyal, first of all, to their own life vision. They explain how this vision integrates into the mission of the organization. By committing themselves to the mission, and letting others see their dedication, leaders inspire others to believe that what they and the organization do makes a difference.

They never—even in the worst of times—deviate from their personal ethics. New leaders are highly principled and hold strong beliefs about their conduct toward the people they manage. They bridge the "trust gap" between employees and bosses by acting with openness and integrity, and staying true to their word.

Stay curious and creative. New leaders are curious—receptive to a variety of ideas and directions, and actively seeking the creativity of others. They challenge tradition, are not afraid of idealism, and have a strong sense of intuition. They embody what the Japanese term *kaizen*— the philosophy of continuous improvement. As such, leaders are always seeking creative ways to improve a product, a process, or themselves.

Keep their focus on people. New leaders believe that people are the most important asset of the business. They stay aware of the changing needs, values, and perceptions of subordinates and staff members. They treat employees with courtesy and respect. They are empathetic, and they sincerely want others to succeed.

The most exciting part of the new leadership is that anyone—regardless of title or function—may have the necessary understanding and skills to lead. In fact, a recent best-selling book by Robert Fulghum suggests that all we really need to know we learned in kindergarten. New leaders, and their organizations, could do worse than abide by Fulghum's schoolyard advice, which includes:

- Play fair.
- Don't hit people.
- Put things back where you found them.
- Clean up your own mess.
- Don't take things that aren't yours.
- When you go out in the world, watch out for traffic, hold hands, and stick together.

NEW ROLES AND RESPONSIBILITIES _____

"Corporations of the future will have to *earn* the loyalty and support of their workers. This will require new ways of managing."
                              —Robert Haas, Chairman, Levi Strauss

Many Americans are seeking employment with companies they can commit to because they want to feel emotionally connected to their work. For most people, loyalty is still an important personal issue. In turn, organizations need the commitment and loyalty of their employees. As Reuben Mark, the CEO of Colgate-Palmolive, has stated: "The essence of business as we move into the 21st century is going to be tapping the talent of good people. It's not about how you locate the plants, it's how you locate the best people and motivate them. It's how you trust them and have them trust you."

As much as we may desire loyalty, however, we all know that the contract has changed. Loyalty today is not what it was twenty years ago. What we need is a new working definition that presents, to both employers and employees, what the new loyalty is, and, just as important, what it is not.

> The new corporate loyalty is
> realistic, candid, and mutual.

Basing loyalty on realistic expectations requires all parties to accept present conditions for what they are, not to bemoan the past ("After all I've done for them . . ."), or dally in utopian fantasy ("In the best of all worlds . . ."). Whether we like it or not, the current reality is that individuals can no longer assume that their jobs are guaranteed, and employers can no longer be assured of an employee's unquestioning dedication. Openly facing these issues, and discussing the forces of change that are driving them, helps people make enlightened decisions about their careers and their commitments.

Managing the new loyalty requires a new set of skills. While managers under the old system could concentrate on output and assume that employees would follow orders without question, the new manager deals with skilled people who have their own ideas on how to do the job. Today's employees are more critical of management, and have objectives of their own which must be taken into consideration. Managers who understand and work with the new realities develop loyalty by encouraging participation and employees' active involvement.

The new loyalty thrives on two-way, honest communication. Employees are candid with their managers when they honestly state their needs and goals, find out what's expected of them, point out areas in the business that need improvement, and offer possible solutions. Employers are candid with employees when they share all the news—good and bad—about developments in the company, and when they keep open lines of communication at all levels of the organization.

The new loyalty is a partnership in which each participant realizes shared goals and responsibilities:

Employees take responsibility for their own careers and well-being. They are loyal, first of all, to themselves. They actively search for work that challenges them, people that inspire them, and companies they can love. When they join an enterprise they commit their best efforts, with the knowledge that serving the organization will ultimately serve their own agendas as well. They display loyalty to the success and performance of a company for as long as they are there.

Organizations attract conscientious people and secure their commitment by communicating an inspired corporate mission that aligns with values held by the work force. Employers acknowledge the mutual nature of loyalty: asking for their employees' creativity, honesty, and willingness to speak up, and in return offering programs and policies that demonstrate trust and respect for all workers. The new loyalty is a partnership in which each participant realizes shared goals and responsibilities.

Joining forces in this partnership can be exhilarating and productive for both employees and employers. As organizational loyalty continues to be examined and redefined, there are great opportunities to create compelling roles and rewards for all parties moving toward a shared vision.

Closing Comments _____

In the months since writing *The Loyalty Factor*, I have been a guest on many radio call-in programs. I recall one radio show in the Northwest, when I was getting an unusual amount of disgruntled employees phoning with their corporate "horror stories." People complained about being unappreciated, underpaid, and misunderstood. They spoke of callous treatment by uncaring bosses, and reported that they worked for indifferent organizations "just interested in making a buck." For the entire hour, all calls followed the same line. Finally, in great disgust, the interviewer asked me: "The principles in your book sound so simple, why aren't more managers following them?"

I thought for a minute. "With all the diet books on the market, why aren't we all thin and trim? What could be simpler than reducing calories and increasing exercise?" The answer to both my question and his is the same. Things that are simple are not necessarily easy.

As a consultant and speaker, I have encountered thousands of employers and employees across America. Never have I met a worker whose life's goal was to do a mediocre job at a company that he or she hated. On the contrary, employees want to do a good job. They want to love their work and to be loyal supporters of their companies. It's more fun.

Never have I encountered a boss who despised all employees. The executives and managers I've met are well-meaning, concerned people. And even if an employer's primary goal were to increase profits, the evidence is conclusive that the way to do so is to empower, loyalize, and care about the well-being of talented employees.

What could be more simple?

As a manager, you know from experience that it may be simple to empower employees, but not at all easy to deal with those workers who don't want to take on the added responsibility. It may be simple—even an inherent part of your nature—to care about the well-being of others, but often far from easy to adequately respond to the variety of individual needs in a highly diversified work force. It may be simple to believe in the principles of loyalty, but difficult to find the time to address, discuss, and resolve these emotionally charged issues (especially in the midst of quarterly quotas and daily crises).

It is no wonder that so many managers struggle, and fail, and question if it is worth the effort. The amazing thing is—in spite of the difficulty—some of you do it so well, you make the simple look easy.

REFERENCES AND RESOURCES

The Affluent Society (John Kenneth Galbraith's book, which defines a new class of workers. Referred to in chapter 4), Houghton Mifflin, 1969.

All I Really Need to Know I Learned in Kindergarten: Uncommon Thoughts on Common Things (Robert Fulghum's best seller, quoted in chapter 5), Villard Books, 1989.

Change-Busting: 50 Ways to Sabotage Organizational Change (management cartoon book from which the illustrations in this book are excerpted), KCS Publishing, P.O. Box 8255, Berkeley, CA 94707, (415) 943-7850.

Creativity in Business (workbook for creative-thinking sessions, mentioned in chapter 3), Crisp Publications, 95 First Street, Los Altos, CA 94022, (415) 949-4888.

InQ Questionnaire (self-assessment instrument discussed in chapter 3), InQ, P.O. Box 10213, Berkeley, CA 94709, (800) 338-2462.

Nordstrom Employee Handbook (the one-page set of rules for employees at the Nordstrom department stores. Quoted in its entirety in chapter 4), Nordstrom, 1501 5th Avenue, Seattle, WA 98101-1603, (206) 628-2111.

Office Support Network (Johnson Wax's personal and professional development program for office support staff, outlined in chapter 4), Margaret D. Plath, Human Resources Manager, OSN Advisor, S. C. Johnson Wax, 1525 Howe Street, Racine, WI 53403, (414) 631-2000.

The 100 Club (employee recognition program outlined in chapter 3), Daniel C. Boyle and Associates, 5–7 Springfield Street, #406, Chicopee, MA 01013, (413) 594-5674.

Passions Within Reason (Robert H. Frank's book, mentioned in chapter 2, which addresses the strategic role of emotions), W. W. Norton, 1988.

Values and Lifestyles Research (SRI's study referred to in chapter 2), Stanford Research Institute, Business Consumers Center, 333 Ravenswood Avenue, Menlo Park, CA 94025, (415) 326-6200.

When Giants Learn to Dance (Rosabeth Moss Kanter's book on mastering the challenges of strategy, management, and careers in the 1990s. Quoted in chapter 5), Simon & Schuster, 1989.

SUGGESTED SUPPLEMENTARY READING

The Change Masters, Rosabeth Moss Kanter, Simon & Schuster, 1984.

Code of the Monarch, Dudley Lynch and Paul L. Kordis, Brain Technologies Corporation, 1990.

Coping with the Fast Track Blues, Robert M. Bramson, Doubleday, 1990.

The Future 500: Creating Tomorrow's Organizations Today, Craig R. Hickman and Michael A. Silva, NAL Books, 1987.

Global Mind Change, Willis Harman, Knowledge Systems, 1988.

The Gold Collar Worker, Robert E. Kelley, Addison-Wesley, 1985.

The Japanese, Peter Tasker, Truman Talley Books, 1988.

Leadership Is an Art, Max DePree, Doubleday, 1989.

Managing for Commitment, Carol Kinsey Goman, Crisp Publications, 1991.

Managing the Equity Factor, Richard C. Huseman and John D. Hatfield, Houghton Mifflin Company, 1989.

Megatrends 2000, John Naisbitt and Patricia Aburdene, William Morrow and Company, 1990.

Trust Me, William J. Morin, Drake Beam Morin, 1990.

The Worth Ethic, Kate Ludeman, E. P. Dutton, 1989.

ABOUT THE AUTHOR

CAROL KINSEY GOMAN, Ph.D., president of Kinsey Consulting Services, is a nationally recognized expert on the "human side" of organizational change. She is an adjunct faculty member at John F. Kennedy University in the M.B.A. program, and serves on the faculty for the United States Chamber of Commerce at its Institutes for Organization Management. From her private counseling practice in Northern California, Dr. Goman helps managers and executives learn to optimize change for personal and organizational advantage. She has written four other books: *Creativity in Business, Executive Renewal: Surviving and Thriving on Change, Managing for Commitment,* and *Change-Busting: 50 Ways to Sabotage Organizational Change.* Addressing conferences and conventions across the United States and Canada, Dr. Goman's upbeat style has earned her a reputation as one of America's best keynote speakers. Her corporate programs are delivered to management and sales groups at client companies that include AT&T, Bank of America, Kaiser Hospitals, and Mrs. Field's Cookies.

Additional copies of *The Loyalty Factor: Building Trust in Today's Workplace* may be ordered by sending a check for $9.95 (please add the following for postage and handling: $1.50 for the first copy, $.50 for each added copy) to:

MasterMedia Limited
16 East 72nd Street
New York, NY 10021
(212) 260-5600
(800) 334-8232

Carol Kinsey Goman is available for keynotes and half-day and full-day seminars. Her topics include: "Thriving on Change in the Nineties," "The Creative Edge," and "The New Corporate Loyalty." Please contact MasterMedia's Speakers' Bureau for availability and fee arrangements. Call Tony Colao at (908) 359-1612.

OTHER MASTERMEDIA BOOKS

THE PREGNANCY AND MOTHERHOOD DIARY: Planning the First Year of Your Second Career, by Susan Schiffer Stautberg, is the first and only updated appointment diary that shows how to manage pregnancy and career. ($12.95 spiralbound)

CITIES OF OPPORTUNITY: Finding the Best Place to Work, Live and Prosper in the 1990's and Beyond, by Dr. John Tepper Marlin, explores the job and living options for the next decade and into the next century. This consumer guide and handbook, written by one of the world's experts on cities, selects and features forty-six American cities and metropolitan areas. ($13.95 paper, $24.95 cloth)

THE DOLLARS AND SENSE OF DIVORCE: The Financial Guide for Women, by Judith Briles, is the first book to combine practical tips on overcoming the legal hurdles with planning finances before, during and after divorce. ($10.95 paper)

OUT THE ORGANIZATION: How Fast Could You Find a New Job?, by Madeleine and Robert Swain, is written for the millions of Americans whose jobs are no longer safe, whose companies are not loyal and who face futures of uncertainty. It gives advice on finding a new job or starting your own business. ($11.95 paper, $17.95 cloth)

AGING PARENTS AND YOU: A Complete Handbook to Help You Help Your Elders Maintain a Healthy, Productive and Independent Life, by Eugenia Anderson-Ellis and Marsha Dryan, is a complete guide to providing care to aging relatives. It gives practical advice and resources to the adults who are helping their elders lead productive and independent lives. ($9.95 paper)

CRITICISM IN YOUR LIFE: How to Give It, How to Take It, How to Make It Work for You, by Dr. Deborah Bright, offers practical advice, in an upbeat, readable and realistic fashion, for turning criticism into control. Charts and diagrams guide the reader into managing criticism from bosses, spouses, children, friends, neighbors and in-laws ($9.95 paper, $17.95 cloth)

BEYOND SUCCESS: How Volunteer Service Can Help You Begin Making a Life Instead of Just a Living, by John F. Raynolds III and Eleanor Raynolds, C.B.E., is a unique how-to-book targeted to business and professional people considering volunteer work, senior citizens who wish to fill leisure time meaningfully and students trying out various career options. The book is filled with interviews with celebrities, CEOs and average citizens who talk about the benefits of service work. ($9.95 paper, $19.95 cloth)

MANAGING IT ALL: Time-Saving Ideas for Career, Family, Relationships and Self, by Beverly Benz Treuille and Susan Schiffer Stautberg, is written for women who are juggling careers and families. Over two hundred career women (ranging from a TV anchorwoman to an investment banker) were interviewed. The book contains many humorous anecdotes on saving time and improving the quality of life for self and family. ($9.95 paper)

REAL LIFE 101: (Almost) Surviving Your First Year Out of College, by Susan Kleinman, supplies welcome advice to those facing "real life" for the first time, focusing on work, money, health and how to deal with freedom and responsibility. ($9.95 paper)

YOUR HEALTHY BODY, YOUR HEALTHY LIFE: How to Take Control of Your Medical Destiny, by Donald B. Louria, M.D., provides precise advice and strategies that will help you to live a long and healthy life. Learn also about nutrition, exercise, vitamins and medication, as well as how to control risk factors for major diseases. ($12.95 paper)

THE CONFIDENCE FACTOR: How Self-Esteem Can Change Your Life, by Judith Briles, is based on a nationwide survey of six thousand men and women. Briles explores why women so often feel a lack of self-confidence and have a poor opinion of themselves. She offers step-by-step advice on becoming the person you want to be. ($9.95 paper, $18.95 cloth)

THE SOLUTION TO POLLUTION: 101 Things You Can Do To Clean Up Your Environment, by Laurence Sombke, offers step-by-step techniques on how to conserve more energy, start a recycling center, choose biodegradable products and proceed with individual environmental cleanup projects. ($7.95 paper)

TAKING CONTROL OF YOUR LIFE: The Secrets of Successful Enterprising Women, by Gail Blanke and Kathleen Walas, is based on the authors' professional experience with Avon Products' Women of Enterprise Awards, given each year to outstanding women entrepreneurs. The authors offer a specific plan to help you gain control over your life and include business tips and quizzes as well as beauty and lifestyle information. ($17.95 cloth)

POWER PARTNERS: How Two-Career Couples Can Play to Win, by Jane Hershey Cuozzo and S. Diane Graham, describes how two-career couples can learn the difference between competing with a spouse and becoming a supportive Power Partner. ($19.95 cloth)

DARE TO CONFRONT! How to Intervene When Someone You Care About Has an Alcohol or Drug Problem, by Bob Wright and Deborah George Wright, shows the reader how to use the step-by-step methods of professional interventionists to motivate drug-dependent people to accept the help they need. ($17.95 cloth)

WORK WITH ME! How to Make the Most of Office Support Staff, by Betsy Lazary, shows how to find, train and nurture the "perfect" assistant and how best to utilize your support staff professionals. ($9.95 paper)

MANN FOR ALL SEASONS: Wit and Wisdom from The Washington Post's *Judy Mann,* by Judy Mann, shows the columnist at her best as she writes about women, families and the politics of the women's revolution. ($19.95 cloth)

THE SOLUTION TO POLLUTION IN THE WORKPLACE,
by Laurence Sombke, Terry M. Robertson and Elliot M.
Kaplan, supplies employees with everything they need to
know about cleaning up their workspace, including recycling, using energy efficiently, conserving water, buying
recycled products and nontoxic supplies. ($9.95 paper)